QUESTAR PUBLISHERS, INC.
Sisters, Oregon

NOT BEFORE... NOT BEHIND...

Stand By

YOUR · MAN

Barb Snyder

STAND BY YOUR MAN
© 1990 by Barb Snyder
Published by Questar Publishers, Inc.

Printed in the United States of America

International Standard Book Number: 0-945564-18-X

To Chuck...my husband, my lover, my friend

CONTENTS

THIS IS THE STORY of two people who married and lived happily ever after...for the most part. Bumps in the road came periodically, sometimes at a faster rate than at other times.

These two people were committed to each other and eventually to Jesus Christ and His way only. This book will tell you about the fun they had, and also the hard times.

Some of the hard times came like sudden blows...some were hard knocks...and some were gentle nudges. Usually the gentle nudges were not felt, and so had to become striking blows to get attention. With each nudge, knock, or blow came the opportunity to prove God and see if doing things His way would really work.

These two people found that His way made each of them a winner. Neither one had to be a loser.

This book is written to show you how we got over the hard times in our marriage — it's OUR story. It's also written to show that it IS possible to enjoy each other along the way.

My prayer all during the writing of this book has been for God to be honored and for His ways to be held high like a banner...a banner that others will follow.

"'Trust in the LORD with all your heart...' It is this state of mind which sets you free." (Oswald Chambers)

NOT BEFORE... NOT BEHIND...

Stand By
YOUR · MAN

HIS
COMMITMENT
&
MINE

...be careful how you walk, not as unwise men, but as wise...
EPHESIANS 5:15

OUR NEW HOUSE was beautiful. The spiral staircase was so graceful as it wound its way around the chandelier that hung from the domed ceiling. The soft rose carpeting brought a warmth to the entryway.

This is the kind of home anyone would like to live in, I thought. And yet, as I wandered through the rooms I kept thinking, *This house means nothing to me as long as Chuck and I are not getting along together.* "Things" were not important when my heart ached to be friends with the one I loved the most.

I felt our new home was separating us. We weren't the same people here that we had been in our other home. There, Chuck had considered me a partner. Now I was supposed to do as he said, and when I didn't agree with him he told me it was "the Lord's will" that I do it. How could I get him to understand we were no longer a team?

Things were not good. I could hardly get up each morning.

I was tired ALL the time. And yet I knew Chuck desired to do what the Lord wanted just as much as I did. We just couldn't agree on what that was!

When we were married, we knew it was for life. Now we were twenty-two years into this marriage — and what a surprise to be so unhappy after all that time. What to do!

Our relationship didn't get better for some time, but because of that lifetime commitment, one evening I put my arms around him as he was sitting at his desk. Leaning over from behind I said, "You know, I don't like you very much right now, but I am completely committed to you. We WILL work this out."

And we did! (That's the subject of our first book — INCOMPATIBILITY: Grounds for a Great Marriage!)

Our commitment — his and mine — was the same. We both wanted the Lord's will. God promised in His Word long ago to lead us in the way we should go. He said, "...be careful how you walk, not as unwise men, but wise" (Ephesians 5:15). The Bible teaches us that the beginning of wisdom is the fear of the Lord (Psalm 111:10). To fear the Lord means to have a wholesome dread or fear of ever displeasing Him. This is how He wants us to walk. So we listened to Him, we obeyed, and we learned. But I want to be sure and say that we did not learn BEFORE we obeyed the Lord, but AFTER. We obeyed when we did not even think it would work. We trusted the Lord...believed that He knew best — and tried *His* way.

Now I stand by my man — not behind, and not before, but by him. I can't do that unless Chuck lets me. At one time Chuck put me behind him. Before I could say "Enough!" he drew me back to his side, and I never had the chance to step out in

front and do things my way only. You see, a woman will usually stay behind her man for only a short time. (By "behind," I
mean that he puts her last in his thinking; he does not consider
her needs, wants, or opinions worthwhile, and does not value
her as an intelligent and talented team member.) SHE knows
she has value, even if he doesn't recognize it. SHE realizes that
she has talents and intelligence that others acknowledge, even
if her husband does not see them. And so...she steps out in
front of him and starts making decisions by herself. If *he*
doesn't care about *her,* then *she* decides not to care about him.

Now she is putting HIM behind HER, and he is confused.
He thinks to himself (and even says to others), "I don't know
what's wrong with that woman. I can't do a thing with her!"

On the other hand, Chuck could not walk by my side if I
did not let him. The decision to walk side by side has to be
made by both partners.

Side by side — that's where the Lord wants husbands and
wives.

I'll tell you how WE do it.

THOUGHTS TO CONSIDER

Are you committed to your mate no matter what?

Have you decided to follow the Lord completely, and without hesitation?

Do you really BELIEVE that God is wisdom, understanding, and knowledge — as the following Scriptures say?

> PROVERBS 1:7
> The fear of the LORD is the beginning of knowledge;
> Fools despise wisdom and instruction.

> PROVERBS 8:13
> The fear of the LORD is to hate evil;
> Pride and arrogance and the evil way,
> And the perverted mouth, I hate.

> PROVERBS 8:14
> Counsel is mine and sound wisdom;
> I am understanding, power is mine.

> PROVERBS 8:17
> I love those who love me;
> And those who diligently seek me will find me.

> PROVERBS 8:19
> My fruit is better than gold, even pure gold,
> And my yield than choicest silver.

Are you willing to obey the Lord, even though you don't feel that what He says to do will work?

Are you willing to walk side by side with your mate, or do you still want to be independent and do your own thing?

SCRIPTURES TO KNOW

EPHESIANS 5:15
...be careful how you walk, not as unwise men, but as wise....

PSALM 111:10
The fear of the Lord is the beginning of wisdom;
A good understanding have all those who do his commandments;
His praise endures forever.

PSALM 112:1
Praise the Lord!
How blessed is the man who fears the Lord,
Who greatly delights in His commandments.

Brethren, I do not regard myself as having laid hold if it yet;
but one thing I do: forgetting what lies behind
and reaching forward to what lies ahead,
I press on toward the goal for the prize
of the upward call of God in Christ Jesus.

PHILIPPIANS 3:13-14

IN MANY WAYS Chuck's past and mine were alike. Our parents had the same values. They took us to Sunday school and church and taught us principles from the Bible at home. They were honest and hard workers, and showed us by example that these were good traits to strive for. They put their families first in their lives, and we always felt we were loved and very special. We both had lots of aunts and uncles and cousins, and our folks made sure we got together with them often.

Chuck's mom was dominant, self-confident, loving, and a great cook, and she sometimes worked outside the home. My mom also was dominant, self-confident, loving, and a great cook, and sometimes worked outside the home.

Chuck's dad helped around the house and took the

garbage out, and my dad also helped around the house and took the garbage out. (Fortunately, therefore, Chuck and I have never had a power struggle in this area). His dad was quiet and didn't talk much. My dad was talkative and no one was a stranger to him.

Chuck was the first-born of three boys. I was the last-born, with three brothers. Even though I was the last-born, I was the only girl, and for that reason — as Kevin Leman describes in his book *The Birth Order Book* — I have the characteristics of a first-born, just like Chuck. Dr. Leman tells us that first-borns want to be in control, and tend to be perfectionists. That's us! Both of us think we are right, and it hasn't been easy to give in to one another.

But in some very important ways our backgrounds were different. In my home, when I was growing up, we said what was on our minds. We did not hold grudges. We talked about what was on our hearts — or at least I did, and because I did, I thought the others did too. (I have since realized this was not always true.)

In Chuck's home, voices weren't raised and feelings were not often shared. Love abounded; anger was seldom expressed. That's not to say there was no anger — it just wasn't shown.

Then, Chuck and I were married.

If we argued or disagreed, Chuck felt we had failed. If we argued or disagreed, I felt we were making progress. I didn't know he was keeping silent to keep peace. It was eleven years before I caught on.

He thought I should be like him. I thought he WAS like me. He didn't say he wasn't, so I thought he was.

When we married, Chuck knew we would be "one" in God's eyes, and he thought *he* was THE one. For a long time I thought he was too.

Chuck's mom cooked a limited variety of food because her men did not like to eat new things. They liked roast beef, mashed potatoes and gravy, macaroni and cheese, bacon and eggs, fried chicken, and "pasties." "Pasties" is a family favorite made with sliced potatoes and onions and diced round steak. You put all this in a rich biscuit dough rolled out and filled like a large turnover, or use pie dough. Line a pie pan with dough, salt and pepper, then dot with butter, and cover with the second crust. Bake for twenty minutes at 425 degrees, then forty-five minutes to an hour at 325 degrees.

(This recipe is very important. I know this because Chuck said he had it written into our marriage vows. In fact, he read it to me from our supposed wedding vows the night we were married, just so I would never forget.)

Chuck's family also liked ham, and chili was a great favorite. I know his mother cooked vegetables, but Chuck says he did not eat them.

My mom cooked a great variety of food, especially lots of home-grown vegetables. In fact, Mom and I ran across a "pasties" recipe in *Sunset* magazine before Chuck and I were married. When he came for dinner soon after, I made them. The only trouble was that the recipe called for carrots to be mixed with the potatoes, onions and steak. I noticed he didn't exactly eat them with relish, but he kept insisting they were wonderful.

It was AFTER we were married that I found out he did not like most cooked vegetables. Before that, each time he was at my parents' home he ate all the vegetables Mom cooked. (He said later he had to eat my mother's cooking in order to "win" me.)

The only vegetables he would eat were corn, peas, and green beans. I cooked mostly his way for fifteen years, but there came a time when I could no longer face corn, peas, and beans; I started cooking a great variety of vegetables just for me.

It's interesting, isn't it, that so much of what we like and do and think is because of our background? Before we are married we never dream the other person is so different. And yet they do not think like we do, they do not eat like we do, and they don't even do things like we do. When going to bed at night, one wants complete silence while the other wants music playing — and not even the kind of music the other one enjoys. Or one may want the window up to let in cold air, while the other cannot stand a cold bedroom. Or one likes a big breakfast in the morning, but the other *never* eats breakfast. And even when both like fried chicken, one likes it soft and steamed, while the other likes it crispy and baked.

Our tendency is to think OUR way of doings things is RIGHT, because that's the way we have always done it. Besides, "Our family turned out good doing it this way — right?"

Having different backgrounds makes me think of Philippians 3:13-14, where the apostle Paul said, "...but one thing I do: forgetting what lies behind and reaching forward to what lies ahead, I press on toward the goal for the prize of the upward call of God in Christ Jesus."

Reaching for the goal and the prize are important to me. I have as my goal to be a godly woman in our marriage. I used to have as my goal to have a happy marriage, but then I realized through some good teaching that I cannot have as my personal goal something that requires the efforts of another person. If my goal involves another person's efforts, then that person may determine whether that goal is reached. I can have a *desire* for a happy marriage, but my *goal* must involve only me. Therefore, to be a godly woman in my marriage is my goal, because it is entirely up to me. It doesn't depend on how Chuck acts, but only on how I act…how I respond to the directions God has given me.

So, after all, it doesn't matter what has happened in our past, be it good or bad. Yes, our past does affect us today, but what I would like to get across is that if my attitude is to learn how God wants me to respond NOW, and I don't keep thinking about the past, but instead forget the past and keep on pressing toward the goals God has for me NOW, then I don't have to be a prisoner of my past.

My focus has to be on obedience to God's Word TODAY, no matter what. If I'm going to be all God wants me to be in this marriage, I have to be learning who Chuck is, what his likes and dislikes are, what makes him tense or nervous, what gives him peace and serenity. He is my most important relationship other than the Lord.

You see, God has given me the supportive role in this marriage, according to 1 Corinthians 11 in which Paul tells us that "man was not created for the woman's sake, but woman for the man's sake. However, in the Lord, neither is woman independent of man nor is man independent of woman." This says that we are indeed in the supportive role, and yet neither husband nor wife can act independently of the other. I'll talk about this more in a later chapter.

I help Chuck the most when I do exactly what the Lord tells me to do for him. So I try not to insist on my own way, and I try (most of the time, that is!) to think more highly of him than myself.

THOUGHTS TO CONSIDER

Are your goals really <u>desires</u>, or can you accomplish your goal with God's help only...with no one else involved?

Do you keep dwelling on the past, and think that you have no power over who you are today?

Have you made a choice to respond in a godly way to life's circumstances?

Have you ever told the Lord Jesus Christ you would follow Him and do things His way? (When you DO tell Him this, He will come into your life and through His Holy Spirit give you the ability to do anything He asks you to do.)

Are you forgetting the past and pressing on, trying to lay hold of that for which you've been laid hold of by Christ?

Do you realize that learning what God has to say in the Bible will equip you for every good work?

Scriptures to Know

2 Timothy 3:16-17
All Scripture is inspired by God and profitable for teaching, for reproof, for correction, for training in righteousness; that the man of God may be adequate, equipped for every good work.

2 Corinthians 3:5
Not that we are adequate in ourselves to consider anything as coming from ourselves, but our adequacy is from God.

2 Corinthians 5:9
Therefore also we have as our ambition...to be pleasing to Him.

...how you turned to God from idols
to serve a living and true God...
1 THESSALONIANS 1:3

WHEN CHUCK AND I MET, I told him I was a Christian.
And I thought I was. After all, I had attended church my whole
life, and I was born in the United States of America. There was
no question that I was a Christian.

Chuck told me he had asked Jesus Christ to come into his
life at a summer Bible camp when he was nine years old. He,
too, had been raised going to church every Sunday. His mom
was the church organist and the church secretary. She had so
many responsibilities there that it took her longer than most
people to leave church on Sundays. Chuck, his dad, and his
brother Jim would sit in the car waiting for her most every Sunday. Chuck tells me that he and Jim would unbutton, untie,
and unzip everything they could on their clothes so that the
moment they arrived home they could change rapidly into
something else and go out to play.

Chuck has to wait for me now on Sundays, just like he

used to wait for his mom. Sometimes I'm sure he's still as anxious to "go out and play" as he was back then.

We started our married life attending church every Sunday. Every time the pastor talked about the Lord coming back for His own, I knew that I was not ready, and yet I didn't know why. When our children were two and three years old I realized I had never invited Jesus Christ into my life, nor told Him I wanted to do things His way. I had never told Him I would follow Him exclusively. I knew He died for the sins of the whole world but I had never personalized it, until one day this realization came to me as I was vacuuming. I stopped, went into our bedroom and got down on my knees, and told the Lord I wanted to follow Him completely. I saw that becoming a Christian was a decision I had to make. I wasn't a Christian just because my mother or grandmother was. I have learned since then that God does not have grandchildren — only children.

Nothing dramatic happened when I prayed that prayer. Yet after that decision I could say the Lord's name without feeling "funny," and I had a compelling desire to learn what the Bible had to say. In fact, I would put the children to bed at 7:30 and start reading the Bible, and not look up until 10:00 or so. (Chuck was working swing shift for a television station during this time, so I had lots of hours to myself in the evening.) It was great to come across things that I had been taught my whole life but did not know where to find in Scripture. It was like getting reacquainted with an old friend. It just felt so comfortable to be with the Lord now. I did not feel the condemnation I used to feel. I felt very peaceful and I knew that I had the Lord's approval.

I was the typical new Christian — so excited by everything I was learning that I came on too strong when telling others about it. For some reason beyond my understanding then, Chuck and I became adversaries when it came to interpreting Scripture. We seldom talked about spiritual things without arguing. If he had a different view than I did, I simply told him he was wrong. I really can't remember, but I probably got out the Bible to prove my point. I didn't understand that man! I thought he should have been as excited as I was! I used to yearn to be able to have an intelligent discussion without it ending in a disagreement. I thought it was all HIS fault that we couldn't discuss Scripture without having a fuss.

I didn't know then what I know today: A man has two fears — the fear of failure, and the fear of being dominated by a woman. (I'll talk about this in detail later.)

So, when I would present something that I had learned to Chuck, subconsciously he had to show that he knew as much or more than I did. I had to learn to back off. As much as I thought I knew, I didn't know that the Bible tells wives to have "a meek and quiet spirit" (1 Peter 3:4). I needed to learn that BEHAVIOR is more important that what is said. I needed to *live* before him more than speak to him (not an easy thing to do for someone who wants to express out loud all that is going on inside). I had not learned yet that God is in control of everything, and that I could relax knowing that He loves Chuck more than I do. God has promised to lead us in the way we should go. It is not MY job to lead Chuck — it is the Lord's job.

In the years since then, I've learned that God has His own ways, and they are not always like mine. I certainly didn't think it was good that I couldn't even talk to my own husband about the Bible, but I knew God said I had to have a quiet spirit about me, so I had to back off. In 1 Peter 3:4, the word translated "quiet" has the meaning in Greek of "keeping your seat." I was not doing that; I was talking as fast as I could and telling Chuck where I thought he was wrong. I had the exact opposite of a quiet spirit; in my spirit I was jumping up out of my chair with a bad attitude, an attitude of "you're wrong and I'm right, and I'm going to make sure you know the 'correct' interpretation; so there!" I did not learn to "keep my seat" for years.

I told the Lord I would do things His way in 1959. It wasn't until 1971 that Chuck and I could talk as one about the Lord. We worked side by side in children's church, and worked hard in our young marrieds' class. We had fun together, we enjoyed each other...but that wonderful spiritual fellowship was not there. We could not talk about the Bible and explore different interpretations, for it always ended in disagreement of some sort. We found it was better to just keep quiet, to keep the peace and not talk. I loved reading books written about the Christian life, and I would ask Chuck to read them too, but he thought they were boring. If I left any books around hoping they might get picked up, I was always disappointed. There just was no interest for him in the things I was reading. On the other hand, I wasn't interested in what Chuck was reading either. We weren't exactly on the same wave length!

THEN, we attended the Basic Youth Conflicts Seminar taught by Bill Gothard. Chuck came away from that week a changed man. We have had great discussions on whether he was saved that week, or just got a new vision. One thing is for sure — he caught the vision for serving others and serving the Lord. Our lives haven't been the same since.

For example, I used to come up with most of the ideas to have people over after church, but after his new commitment I could hardly keep up with all the invitations he wanted to extend. He started caring more for other people than he did for his own time.

At the beginning of this chapter I quoted from 1 Thessalonians 1:3. The apostle Paul was telling how everyone he came in contact with had heard that the Thessalonian believers had turned to God from idols to serve a living and true God. In these words Paul was implying that idols are not living, nor do they give you truth. Only "the living and true God" can give us what we are looking for in the idols.

We don't use the word *idols* very much today, but we still worship them. One idol may be money; we focus on making money and spending money. Another idol may be ourselves — "What can I do or get for *me?* How can I make *me* happy? What will bring pleasure to *me?*" Another idol may be "my time." We don't want to get involved in too many outside things or get involved with other people because they rob us of the time we've reserved for ourselves.

Anything that keeps us from doing what God wants, anything that takes our time or our attention away from the Lord in a continuous way, is an idol. When the Lord says to discipline ourselves for godliness, and we instead spend more time disciplining ourselves physically, then that physical exercise, even though it is good, can be an idol that is keeping us from godliness. (I'm not saying that we cannot exercise; I'm saying that if it comes BEFORE God, then it is an idol.)

When Chuck saw that the Lord wanted us to put Him and others first, just as the Thessalonians did, then our lives really changed. The spiritual concerns that used to be on MY timetable switched to HIS timetable.

I'm not an idea person, but Chuck's ideas never stop — he begins almost every sentence with "I've been thinking..." So with his new spiritual concern for others, suddenly I was on the fast track instead of my own leisurely pace.

Chuck and I have the same goal, and that is to be obedient

and to glorify the Lord in all our ways. But there is one problem. Chuck often has different plans than I do AND wants to do them in a different way. He just plain thinks differently than I do. So we have decided together not to do anything unless we both agree. (I'll tell you how we arrived at this decision in the chapter "His Goals and Mine.")

For both of us, our faith no longer is just in our heads, but in our hearts also. When our hearts were changed, our whole motive for living was changed. Our desires for the comforts of life are still there, but over and above those desires we each have individual goals to be all that the Lord wants us to be. We want to walk pleasing to Him.

In 2 Peter 1:5, God tells us to supply moral excellence to our faith. And He tells us to do this with "all diligence." In other words, we are to work hard at supplying this characteristic. Moral excellence means doing things that are pleasing to God, and it means *fulfilling your intended purpose.* It means *excellence with energy.* Another word for moral excellence is *virtue.*

Moral excellence is what Jesus Christ is. When He came to earth, he *fulfilled the purpose for which He came.*

It's like this: Let's say you buy an apple tree and have every expectation that it will give you big, juicy apples. But it doesn't produce — or if it does, the apples are small and don't ripen before they drop off the tree. We can say that this tree is not morally excellent.

Another example may be a farmer who buys a field, expecting to cultivate a good crop on it. But the ground does not fulfill the purpose for which it was intended. It grows weeds easily, but the planted crop never lives up to expectations. That field has no moral excellence, no virtue. That field is not pleasing to the farmer.

As I said, Chuck and I want to be pleasing to the Lord. We want to fulfill the purpose for which we were intended. There are so many things we were intended to be, but first and foremost, as Romans 8:29 says, we are predestined to become conformed to the image of Jesus Christ. We want to be just like Jesus Christ, who did only those things that were pleasing to the Father. We desire more than anything in the world to walk pleasing to Him, and we stand by each other in this.

THOUGHTS TO CONSIDER

Have you considered that everything coming into your life comes from God, whether you think it is good or bad? (This realization is the definition of "meekness," a fruit of the Spirit.)

When things aren't going your way, do you have that meek and quiet spirit that is so pleasing to the Lord?

Meekness and a quiet spirit are pleasing to the Lord because they show that you recognize He is Ruler over all...that He is in control of all things...that He is sovereign.

Are you supplying moral excellence to your faith, or are you still determined to please yourself more than please the Lord?

SCRIPTURES TO KNOW

2 PETER 1:2-8

Grace and peace be multiplied to you in the knowledge of God and of Jesus our Lord; seeing that His divine power has granted to us everything pertaining to life and godliness, through the true knowledge of Him who called us by His own glory and excellence.

For by these He has granted to us His precious and magnificent promises, in order that by them you might become partakers of the divine nature, having escaped the corruption that is in the world by lust.

Now for this very reason also, applying all diligence, in your faith supply moral excellence, and in your moral excellence, knowledge; and in your knowledge, self-control, and in your self-control, perseverance, and in your perseverance, godliness; and in your godliness, brotherly kindness, and in your brotherly kindness, Christian love.

For if these qualities are yours and are increasing, they render you neither useless nor unfruitful in the true knowledge of our Lord Jesus Christ.

HIS WALK & MINE

> ...so that you may walk in a manner worthy of the Lord,
> to please Him in all respects, bearing fruit in every good work
> and increasing in the knowledge of God...
> COLOSSIANS 1:10

CHUCK ASKED ME one time what I thought "the deep things of the Word" were. I thought for a while and said that one deep thing would be seeing how God wants us to serve others. In our way of reasoning, we think we will get what we want out of life if we serve OURSELVES. We want to make sure we are "first," but God's secret is that if we serve others, they will respond to us the way we wanted them to in the first place.

After Chuck said he agreed with me (I nearly fainted from shock), we discussed it further. We remembered the Lord's summary of the Ten Commandments, telling us to love the Lord with all our heart, with all our mind, with all our soul, and with all our strength, and our neighbor as ourselves (Mark 12:30-31). Because *love* is an action verb, this Scripture is probably the best definition of serving. No one knows he is loved by us unless we DO something for him, unless we act out our love — and that is *serving.* Too often we refuse to humble ourselves to show love, because we want others to serve US and love US.

Another verse that describes serving is Matthew 7:12 — "Therefore whatever you want others to do for you, do so for them...."

In 1 Corinthians 13 we are given a pattern to follow, a pattern that shows us how to "do for others." Let me quote the passage for you:

> Love is patient, love is kind, and is not jealous; love does not brag and is not arrogant, does not act unbecomingly; it does not seek its own, is not provoked, does not take into account a wrong suffered, does not rejoice in unrighteousness, but rejoices with the truth; bears all things, believes all things, hopes all things, endures all things. Love never fails....

This is how the Lord wants us to do for others what we want them to do for us. This is how we are to serve others.

It's the same thing Paul told us in Philippians 2 —

> Do nothing from selfishness or empty conceit, but with humility of mind let each of you regard one another as more important than himself; do not merely look out for your own personal interests, but also for the interests of others.

I have watched Chuck since the Lord spoke to his heart about serving God and others. He has acted out that principle. He came away from that seminar with a commitment to serve. He is more patient, and less self-centered. Before his commitment to serve, he wanted things his way. But afterward, he started putting the interests of others before his own. Before, if he was working and someone interrupted him, it was an irritation because he thought what he was doing was more important. But after his commitment to serve, his values changed.

I worked for Chuck for a short time as his secretary, receptionist, and media buyer. Our advertising agency was small at the time, so I could handle all those jobs. One day someone dropped in unexpectedly just to talk to Chuck. He stayed and stayed and stayed. I knew Chuck would be beside himself. Of course, he would be nice and patient when his guest was with him, but I knew I would hear about it after he was gone. But afterwards Chuck was just as relaxed as he was before his guest came. I couldn't understand what had happened to him. He told me he had learned that "circumstances are temporary, but people are eternal." He had changed his attitude, and decided to serve.

After the Bill Gothard seminar, I don't know that I thought all that much about serving. I was struck more with the thought that God was in complete control of my life. Some time later I learned about the fruit of the Spirit called "meekness," and sometimes translated "gentleness" (Galatians 5:22-23). I learned that it is seeing God in control of every area of my life. I learned that God rules over all, and because He does I do not have to worry about anything! I can have a serenity of spirit no matter what the circumstances. I learned that the circumstances do not have to control me, but with God's help I can control myself despite circumstances. It is like being a thermostat instead of a thermometer. A thermostat controls the circumstances, but a thermometer goes up and down with the circumstances.

To be *meek* in a biblical sense is to cause no disturbance to those around me because I recognize that God causes ALL things to work together for good. It is knowing that God is FOR me, therefore who can be against me? (Romans 8:28-31)

In other words, there is not a circumstance involving people, places or things that God has not allowed, and even though I don't like something and consider it a hard trial, I know God is in control.

As I've written this about meekness, I've realized that we really have to KNOW what God says about Himself in the Bible to be able to live this way. And even more than that, we have to BELIEVE what He is saying. Sometimes I think that people believe God can save them and take them to heaven, but they don't believe Him for their everyday walk. They don't believe Him when He says that if they do things His way, He will take care of them (Matthew 6:33).

So what about Chuck's walk and mine? As I said before, my life has never been the same since Chuck's total commitment to the Lord. He wants to serve others, and because he is an "idea" person his ideas for serving never stop. And his ideas usually involve me in some way. Let me give you an example.

When we first moved into the big home we live in now, I felt Chuck was inviting everyone over for everything. We had business groups, church groups, college groups, Campus Crusade for Christ groups, Youth for Christ groups, high school groups, junior high groups, family groups, Bible study groups, and groups and groups and groups.

In Chuck's joy of sharing this house with others, he forgot that I did not feel well, and that I would have to be the one getting the house ready and preparing the food for them. Of course, many times they would bring their own food in, but I still wanted and needed to be there to supervise and help them with finding my dishes and with serving. I needed to be a good hostess.

I was also teaching my Precept Bible Study group during this time and working for Chuck at the office doing all the finances (I had been promoted from secretary and reception-ist). I was also playing tennis twice a week, and trying to deco-rate the house. Chuck and I were also teaching a class on Sunday mornings as well as two other Bible study groups. With all the teaching we were doing, I needed to study at least two hours a day. During this time we also had many overnight guests, and some were going through heavy trials and needed to talk about them.

The ONLY way I knew to cope with all this was to see that God was still in control of what was happening around me. It seemed that CHUCK was in control, but I knew that actually it was God.

This time was not easy, and my attitude was not good many, many, many (most) times. This was in the days before we knew that unless we both agreed on what we should do, we did not do anything. It was also before we realized that marriage is not a hierarchy, but rather a team effort. But I HAD learned that God was in control. I did not know how it could work out for my good (surely God couldn't want anyone to be as tired as I was), but I had to trust the Lord, even though I felt hopeless.

On the other hand, Chuck was feeling hopeless too. After all, the Lord had given us this home, and Chuck believed it should be used constantly to serve others; in this way he was serving the Lord too.

It was hard for both of us, and yet even then our goal was to walk in a manner that was worthy of the Lord. We both wanted to please Him first and foremost. We learned that even when things are not going our way we must keep our focus on the Lord. We learned that the important thing is not "why" we are going through a trial, but "how" we go through it. We had to keep asking the Lord for wisdom, just like it says in the first chapter of James. As I said earlier, we've got to know what the Scripture says so we can do it. We make so many messes for ourselves because we are ignorant; we just do not know what the Lord says to do in various situations.

I was talking to my friend Dayna about writing this book. We were talking about husbands of course, and about the times we do not agree with something they have done or want us to do. Dayna said, "You know, when your husband is disobedient to God, you have to treat him just as if he were not saved. You have to reverence him and all that stuff!"

We laughed — but I was so glad that she knew what "reverence and all that stuff" was. Most wouldn't even know enough to make such a statement. Dayna knows that to do the will of the Lord doesn't always feel good, but she knows that 1 Peter 3:1 tells us to be an example of godly BEHAVIOR to our husbands instead of trying to "tell" them where they are wrong. And she also knows that to reverence your husband is to have a reluctance to displease him. In other words, we are to put the interests of our husbands ahead of our own. And that takes us back to the theme of serving.

When I talk about our walk with the Lord, I am talking about our actions BECAUSE of our faith. Our actions will be based on what we believe, and our belief is based on what the Bible says. Our actions will also be determined by our attitude. Are our responses because we love the Lord with all our heart or because we love *ourselves* with all our hearts?

When the Lord gives us directions to live by, He does it so we can serve and love one another. And when we follow His directions we are serving, loving, and honoring Him. As Colossians 1:10 tells us, our responsibility is to walk in a manner worthy of the Lord, to please Him in all respects, bearing fruit in every good work and increasing in the knowledge of God, NO MATTER WHAT IS GOING ON AROUND US. Our motivation for this walk must consciously be to honor and glorify the Lord. We should not walk to please ourselves, or to make ourselves look good, or to use our walk as a means to get what WE want. Our motivation — our heart attitude — must be to honor and glorify the Lord because He IS the Lord.

So...the only way I know to stand by your man in his walk with the Lord is to be obedient yourself — to be obedient to the things you know the Lord would have you do. And the only way you can find out what HE wants you to do is to study the Bible, and obey what it says.

So there's your answer. Simple...but hard!

THOUGHTS TO CONSIDER

Do you know that the main message of the Bible is for us to love God and love others?

Have you ever equated loving with serving?

When you think of loving others, do you automatically think of doing something for them that will make THEM feel special?

Have you studied the Bible enough to KNOW how the Lord wants you to act towards Him and others?

Have you ever made it your goal to study the Bible?

Have you equated loving God with obedience to His commands?

Scriptures to Know

John 14:15
If you love Me, you will keep My commandments.

John 14:21
He who has My commandments, and keeps them, he it is who loves Me; and he who loves Me shall be loved by My father and I will love him, and will disclose Myself to him.

John 15:16
You did not choose Me, but I chose you, and appointed you, that you should go and bear fruit....

Colossians 1:10
...so that you may walk in a manner worthy of the Lord, to please Him in all respects, bearing fruit in every good work and increasing in the knowledge of God....

HIS *LOVE* & MINE

Therefore be imitators of God, as beloved children; and walk in love,
just as Christ also loved you, and gave Himself up for us,
an offering and a sacrifice to God as a fragrant aroma.

EPHESIANS 5:1-2

THE DAY WE WERE MARRIED, I'm sure we both thought the
other person was going to make us happy. And it was true for
a while. After our wedding ceremony we drove to the Seattle
area. We spent the first night alone, then drove on to Tacoma
to spend that night with Chuck's folks. His grandmother was
ill, and we wanted to see her and show ourselves off. On the
third day we drove back over the mountains to my hometown,
Wenatchee, Washington. We spent that night with my folks.
We went through our wedding presents and exchanged some
of our fourteen casseroles for a dish rack and pans and items
like that.

On our way to Wenatchee that day, Chuck looked at me
and with all seriousness said, "What's all this *adjusting* people
talk about? We're not having problems!" We thought we were
so smart, and life would always be happy and problem-free.

We didn't know that it's not when things go well, but when things are not so good that the adjusting needs to be done.

On the fifth day of our honeymoon Chuck and I drove back to college to really start our life together. We were married in between semesters and had only a few days before classes would begin again.

Chuck finished his senior year, and I finished my sophomore year. It was like playing house. We had a tiny little apartment with a pull-down bed in the living room. The room was so small that every piece of furniture had to be moved in order to get the bed down.

In about two months I felt sick to my stomach every morning. Chuck would bring me soda crackers (they seemed to help) and kept telling me that if I would only get well, we could start a family. We did not know our family was already started.

Tim came ten months and four days after we were married. He was born in New Jersey, at Fort Monmouth, because by this time Chuck was in the United States Army.

When Tim was fourteen days old, my mother and I took a train to Fayetteville, North Carolina, where Chuck had gone to find a place for us to live. He was to be stationed there at Fort Bragg for the rest of our two years in the Army.

About nine months before Chuck was to be discharged from the service, I got sick to my stomach in the mornings again. Bev was born the day before Chuck was discharged. I had flown back to Washington two months earlier, and with travel time allowed by the Army, Chuck arrived in time for Bev's birth.

Back together again, we lived first with my folks, then his folks, then my folks while Chuck worked at my uncle's apple-packing-and-storage warehouse. When that seasonal work was over we lived with his folks again until Chuck started his television career at KING-TV in Seattle. Chuck worked there for most of eleven years. He started out as a floor director — that means he was the one who stood beside the camera man and gave time signals to the on-air personalities. He also made up sets and took them down again.

As he progressed in the company he directed the Evening News Hour and news documentaries. He often helped an advertiser with the grocery commercials, and when the time came for Chuck to make a career change, this man hired him for his advertising agency.

Through all the years I've loved Chuck so much. I haven't always liked him, but I have always loved him. Let me explain. It's okay not to always like a person, because love does not include having to like someone. You see, love is a commitment that has nothing to do with feelings. I wish everyone could understand this, because we can't possibly like someone all the time. Love is action, not feelings, and it is out of that action that our feelings come. It was (and is) during those times when I don't especially "like" Chuck that my commitment to love him has held me steadfast to our marriage vows.

In *The Kink and I*, Dr. James Mallory says, "Love is an act of the will which may or may not be accompanied by a state of mind. Love is a commitment, a commitment of our wills."

He also says, "Love means, 'I will give you love when I feel like it, when I don't feel like it, and until I do feel like it.'"

I am just amazed sometimes at how much I feel "in love" with Chuck. Then, in another instance, I don't like him at all, because of something he says or doesn't say, something he does or doesn't do. I don't know, but the feelings flee and I'm still married to him. What a freeing thing to know that it's okay to lose the feeling, but I never have to lose my commitment to him!

I have found through hard times that the best thing I can do for Chuck is to make him FEEL loved. So I asked him recently what I do for him, other than the obvious, that he likes the most. He said, "I like it when you play with me, when we have fun together." I was just amazed, for the Bible tells me that my job is to love him with a friendship/flirty/playful love. My love for him is to make him feel admired and special. I'm SUPPOSED to play with him. I'm SUPPOSED to have fun with him. I'm SUPPOSED to make him feel special.

I have a harder time with teasing and playing than Chuck does. He loves to joke and tease and have fun. One day long ago I read somewhere that we must not only be consumers of happiness, but producers also. I've tried to do that ever since. I used to just soak up all his happiness and not produce much for him. I was always too busy to be playful. I was cleaning the house and raising the children and talking on the phone and knitting, or whatever else I thought was important. And yet, the most important thing I can do for Chuck is to show him I like him by having fun with him — to show him that he is my friend, not just my husband. When I enjoy him, he KNOWS I love him.

When we were in the army stationed in New Jersey, I started to tell him that I loved him, and it came out "I like you." We both laughed and thought it was funny. We didn't know then that the Bible had already told me to like him.

For years, Chuck had me on a performance basis. That is, I had to do things the way he wanted and I had to agree with his opinions, or I did not receive his approval. He didn't know that he was told to love me unconditionally, that no matter how he thought I should act, I did not have to perform for him. He is to love me just because I am precious in God's sight. He is to love me as Christ loves the church and gave Himself up for her.

One way I had to perform was to keep my voice sounding a certain way or I would get disapproval. Whenever we had a disagreement and my voice would get higher and louder in our discussions, he would cut off our talks by saying, "You should just hear yourself!" Then he would turn around and walk away. You see, I had to talk and sound right before he would listen to me. I didn't know how hard communication was for him during a conflict, and he didn't know how much I needed to talk out the problems I thought we were having. When I suspected that any moment he could walk away, I started talking faster, and with more emotion, and louder.

To love me unconditionally, like God loves me, would have made Chuck stay and listen and talk, no matter how I sounded. And to love him the way I should would be to remain calm, and to build him up by giving him the benefit of the doubt instead of tearing him down and accusing him of whatever I thought he had done. I wish we had known then what we know now about communication. (I'll talk more about it in the chapter "His Communication and Mine.")

You know how you try to do everything you can to please a friend. You plan times together, you send thoughtful notes, you buy little gifts from time to time and you say nice, kind things. That is what we wives are to do for our husbands. In fact, that is how we are told to love our children also. This kind of love is called *phileo* love in the Bible. Titus 2:4 tells us older women to encourage the young women to love their husbands, and to love their children. The word for love in Titus 2:4 is *phileo.*

This kind of love can also be defined this way: It is to have a fondness for other people, to be attracted to them so that you make fun for them and with them. This love for your husband would make you want to flirt with him and laugh with him as you look into his eyes with admiration. And because you value him so highly, you praise him and pay attention to him.

Phileo love is a responding love. You see something in another person that attracts you. Greek scholar Kenneth Wuest says, "It is a love that is called out of one's heart as a response to the pleasure one takes in a person or object."

It's like this: When you first met your husband-to-be he let you know he was attracted to you. You thought, *My, he has good sense. I think he's pretty nice too.* Then you treated each other with kindness and you each responded to the other. As time went on and you found common interests and shared yourselves with one another (always being thoughtful of each other), you decided you could commit yourself to him. After all...anyone who thinks you're so attractive wouldn't be hard to live with at all. In fact, you could have a wonderful life with someone who thinks you are so intelligent and who prizes your opinions so much. He even thinks you are fun to be with, so you will obviously live happily ever after! And besides, you think the same thing about him!

You responded to each other. You did what the Lord says to do: to treat others the way you want to be treated yourself.

But — after marriage comes commitment. And that commitment can be explained by another Greek word.

Wives are told specifically to love their husbands with *phileo* love, yet husbands are never told in the Bible to love their wives with this kind of love. Rather, husbands are told to love their wives with *agape* love.

Wuest describes *agape* love as "a love that is called out of one's heart by the preciousness of the object loved. It is a love of esteem, of evaluation. It has the idea of prizing. It is the most noble word for love in the Greek language." This love does not depend on what the other person does. It is not a love of response, but a love that depends on the character of the one doing the loving. This kind of love is a choice. It is a choice you make by thinking right about the Lord and about the object of your love. When you choose to love with this kind of love, it is because you know the other person is precious in God's sight. Therefore you CHOOSE to make this person precious in your sight also.

When I studied this word in my Precept Bible Study *Marriage Without Regrets,* I found that *agape* love is not kindled by the merit or worth of its object, but originates in its own God-given nature. Scripture says that God is love — that is, God is *agape* love. Further, this kind of love delights in giving, and keeps on loving even when the loved one is unresponsive, unkind, unlovable, and unworthy. It is unconditional love. *Agape* love desires only the good of the one loved. It is a consuming passion for the well-being of others. Therefore it is a decision to give value to another.

Ephesians 5:25 tells husbands, "Love your wives, just as Christ also loved the church and gave Himself up for her." The structure of this verse in the Greek is in the present tense, the imperative mood, and the active voice. This sounds complicated, but it simply means, "Keep on loving as a habit of life...this is a command...and the husband is responsible to initiate this love toward his wife."

I think the reason God told wives to love their husbands with a love that makes them feel admired and prized is so husbands can more easily choose and initiate unconditional love. On the other hand, when our husbands love us unconditionally, we can more easily love them with a friendship/flirty love.

It sounds like God knew what He was doing!

Even though wives are NOT specifically given instructions to love their husbands with *agape* love, we are told to love our brothers and sisters in the Lord that way. Ephesians 5:1-2 tells us to "be imitators of God, as beloved children; and walk in love, just as Christ also loved you and gave Himself up for us, an offering and a sacrifice to God."

Also, in John 15:12-13 the Lord Jesus tells us, "This is My commandment, that you love one another, just as I have loved you. Greater love has no one than this, that one lay down his life for his friends."

When Jesus used the word *friends* here, He was talking about those who are in covenant with one another. We are in covenant with our husbands, for that is what marriage is. We are also in covenant with the Lord.

To be in covenant means that you have made a solemn, binding agreement to become one with another. Your strength is your partner's strength, and your partner's strength is yours. You become completely identified with your covenant partner, never again to live independently. What concerns your covenant partner concerns you, and vice versa. When we enter into covenant with the Lord Jesus Christ we become completely identified and one with Him, because God gives us the Holy Spirit to live within us. And since God is love and He lives within us, we have the power to love exactly the way He tells us to. His identity becomes our identity, His strength our strength, His love our love.

Therefore, all that I've told you about loving your partner is possible through your covenant with Jesus Christ. Whether you choose to love with an affectionate responding love or with an initiating unconditional love, God will enable you — and has already enabled you, because Jesus Christ has prayed for you "that the love wherewith Thou didst love Me may be in them, and I in them" (John 17:26). With God's enabling, you and I can love *His* way.

God showed us how to love. He loved us so much that He gave…. So, as I have said, love is not a feeling; it is giving something of yourself so the other person feels loved. We would never have known how much God loved us if He had not sent His only Son to give up His life for us. He is our example of how to love — which, after all, is giving.

The best part of choosing to love one another whether we feel like it or not is that the feelings WILL come as others respond to our loving, and we respond to their response.

Here's an example: Chuck seemed very quiet one Saturday. I asked him what was wrong, but he said nothing was; he just had a bad headache. I thought to myself that he'd had a headache before and still talked to me and treated me nicely, but I let it go.

The weekend continued in this way until I finally said some angry things and accused him of ruining the whole weekend by his attitude. Then I felt convicted about the things I had said.

Chuck went to work on Monday without anything being settled. However, when he called from work I decided to act like nothing had happened, and in effect to be kind instead of distant. He said later it was because of my attitude that he said, "Let's go out to dinner tonight to talk." Unknown to me, he had gotten up earlier than usual and gone out to breakfast by himself. I thought he'd had a breakfast meeting. He spent the time at breakfast writing down everything that I had been doing (or that he THOUGHT I had been doing) that had recently been driving him crazy.

At dinner that night we talked about everyday things until after we had eaten. Then he pulled out a thick sheaf of papers and told me he had written down everything he was troubled about. His list looked so long, I thought I would be dead by the time we got through it. However, because we had both decided to be open with each other (which is the same as being kind and loving), we went through his list one by one. On some things I had to agree with Chuck and ask forgiveness, but on others I could say that, no, that was not what I was thinking, and I didn't mean it that way, and I explained what I DID mean.

By the end of the list we were better friends and loved each other more than when the whole thing started.

So at first when Chuck was moody, I responded correctly; but that soon turned to anger and I let him know about it. Then we were both angry. But since love is a commitment to the other person to treat him in a loving way, I went back to being nice to Chuck and caused him to respond in the same way. The outcome was good communication, which is a loving thing to do, instead of continued war.

Once again the Lord proved Himself faithful, for according to Scripture you will receive just as much love as you give — "Therefore whatever you want others to do for you, do so for them; for this is the Law and the Prophets" (Matthew 7:12).

When we think of what true love is, the best place to see it described may well be 1 Corinthians 13. Here it is again:

Love is patient, love is kind, and is not jealous; love does not brag and is not arrogant, does not act unbecomingly; it does not seek its own, is not provoked, does not take into account a wrong suffered, does not rejoice in unrighteousness, but rejoices with the truth; bears all things, believes all things, hopes all things, endures all things. Love never fails....

I'd like to take these principles one by one and try to explain them, as well as give you an example that will match each thing that love is.

"Love Is Patient"

Love is longsuffering. It does not give up. It refuses to be provoked or angered even by insults. It is tolerant and able to wait calmly for something desired.

If I had been patient with Chuck when he was not talking to me, I would not have spit out angry words at him after being patient for most of the weekend. I SHOULD have talked to him about our problem, but not in an angry way. I could have asked him to think about what was wrong, and then we could talk about it later. I did not patiently wait for God to work in his life. I took matters into my own hands.

"Love Is Kind"

This kind of love treats others as you want to be treated. It is sympathetic, friendly, gentle, tenderhearted, generous, cordial, affectionate, and on and on. The list could be endless because of what is called for in different situations.

Last night, because of a busy day, I did not have dinner completed when Chuck arrived home. He came in and sat down in the rocking chair in the kitchen. We visited as I prepared dinner. He decided to feed our kitty and had to get a clean dish. When he saw that the dishwasher had not been emptied, he unloaded it for me. Because of his kindness I felt he loved me. His kindness showed me he understood that I was tired.

"Love Is Not Jealous"

Love is not resentfully suspicious of another or of another's influence. It does not require exclusive loyalty.

Chuck and I each have many friends and we realize that we bring interest to our own relationship because of our other relationships. It's fun to hear about his conversations with others, and he feels the same way about mine. We are not jealous of one another's friendships.

"Love Does Not Brag"

Love does not flaunt or boast about itself.

I think it's possible to tell your mate about what is happening in your life in a way that may sound like boasting if you were to say the same thing to an acquaintance. If it is truth, then love rejoices in the truth.

"Love Does Not Act Unbecomingly"

Love does not act inappropriately nor unattractively. It is not indecorous.

This kind of love would not show anger to one another in public, or do anything to embarrass one another. So, when either Chuck or I feel the other other is incorrect in something that is said in public, we wait until we're home to discuss it. We try not to do anything to make the other look inadequate in front of others.

"Love Does Not Seek Its Own"

Love is not selfish. The person who loves is not out for himself.

Jesus Christ is our perfect example, for when He came to

earth to love us by dying for us He gave up His rights to benefit Himself, and took on the appearance and form of a man.
He did not use His rights as the God of the universe to benefit
Himself. He did not seek His own way. He did not seek to be
served, but instead He served us.

"Love Is Not Provoked"

Love is not provoked to anger or irritation. It isn't even
annoyed.

This love simply accepts people as they are, and remem-
bers that God rules over all and has allowed each circumstance to come into our lives.

Wouldn't it be wonderful if we could be like this all the
time, and live with someone who had this attitude! I've seen
Chuck decide not to be irritated or annoyed even though in the
flesh that would be his natural reaction. Then, too, I've seen
him get really irritated and show it...like this week. He was so
angry because the restaurant where we meet for the Mariners
baseball team Bible study forgot we were scheduled, and we
had to walk through a meeting of about one hundred women to
get to our room. Then we couldn't open the sliding door. When
we finally got it open, we couldn't close it. Pianos were playing
in two adjoining rooms, and to top it off, the intercom started
playing music in our room. The tables were not properly set up
either (they had actually been set up in case the women's meeting needed them). When Chuck spoke to the manager, they
misunderstood each other because they were both angry, irritated, and annoyed. Even though Chuck appeared calm, his
clipped sentences and tense jaw let us all know that he was
bothered. In fact, one of the ball players was quite tickled about
it because he had never seen Chuck angry before.

Chuck did not come through with flying colors at the restaurant, but afterward he realized he had shown that he was provoked, and wrote the manager a letter of apology. As Chuck teaches, each time we fail it is an opportunity to make it right by being obedient and humbling ourselves by doing things the Lord's way. In a situation like this, the Lord wants us to ask for forgiveness. Chuck really is a wonderful example to me. (By the way, the manager also wrote back a kind and loving response to Chuck's letter. Because Chuck showed love by asking forgiveness, he received back love in response.)

"Love Does Not Take into Account a Wrong Suffered"

This love does not even notice offenses, because it is concentrating so hard on the Lord and others.

"Love Does Not Rejoice in Unrighteousness"

Unrighteousness is what is wrong, wicked, sinful, unfair, unjust. I think we rejoice in unrighteousness when we enjoy watching television programs or movies that show all these things. We need to keep our minds free from unrighteousness. To watch movies that exalt immorality (such as men and women living together without marriage, and having babies out of wedlock) without even realizing that we are rejoicing in unrighteousness is common. We often just accept things as they are presented, and do not even perceive that we are rejoicing in unrighteousness.

"Love Rejoices with the Truth"

Truth is trustworthiness, genuineness, honesty, and reality. It is agreement with a standard or rule, and of course that standard is the Word of God. It is correctness and accuracy — that which agrees with fact or reality.

In John 17:17, Jesus prays, "Thy word is truth." Anything that does not line up with the Word of God is not truth. That is why we need to know the Bible so well. We need to be able to discern the counterfeit.

"Love Bears All Things"

The ability to withstand rough treatment is a love that bears all things. This love is rugged, tough, and determined.

This is the most striking characteristic of *agape* love. This is the kind of love that God loves us with while we were still sinners, enemies, ungodly, and helpless, as Romans 5:3-5 tells us.

"Love Believes All Things"

When one believes, he has confidence in a statement or promise of another person.

This is the kind of love we need for the Lord. We must have confidence to believe His promises and His commands. God is faithful to His Word, and if He tells us there will be a consequence to disobedience, we have to believe that, just as much as we have to believe there will be a blessing for obedience.

"Love Hopes All Things"

Hope is the feeling that what is wanted will happen. We have hope because we trust. Despite a situation seeming to have no basis for hope, we hope nevertheless.

Romans 5:5 reminds us that "hope does not disappoint;

because the love of God has been poured out within our hearts through the Holy Spirit who was given to us."

Doing things His way lets us hope with assurance because we know His Word is truth, and when God says He will be faithful to us, He *is* faithful to us.

"Love Endures All Things"

Enduring love holds up under pain or fatigue. Even though life is hard, we are to stand, to bear up, to undergo, to put up with it and to tolerate it in a God-honoring way.

The only way we can do this is to believe and understand that God is in control of all circumstances of our life. This is where the Spirit-fruit *meekness* comes into reality. We can keep on loving with endurance because our God does not let us go through anything that is not for our ultimate good. Scripture tells us that God is loving and good, and along with His love and goodness He is also merciful (1 John 4:8, Psalm 106:1, Psalm 116:5). Knowing this, we can endure with confidence.

"Love Never Fails"

Love is never without strength. Love that is given as God loves will always be powerful. There will never be an insufficiency nor lack in love. Love never stops operating; therefore we CAN bear all things, believe all things, hope all things, and endure all things.

To realize that love never fails is astounding. This is a fact. We just need to endure long enough and keep on loving long enough to see the truth of it.

For the most part, Chuck and I have a quiet, calm home where lots of kind things are said, where sweet things are done for each other, where we are trying to put the other first. Of course we fail, and become self-centered instead of giving, but we have learned that maturity is not being without disagreements; rather, maturity is how fast we get over disagreements and become friends and lovers again.

The reason we want to show love and kindness to one another is because our goal in life is to be imitators of God — to walk in love, just as Christ also loved us and gave Himself up for us, an offering and a sacrifice to God, as a fragrant aroma.

Noted Bible teacher Oswald Chambers said this:

There is only one Being who loves perfectly, and that is God, yet the New Testament distinctly states that we are to love as God does; so the first step is obvious. If ever we are going to have perfect love in our hearts we must have the very nature of God in us.

When I am possessed by God it is not that He gives me power to love like He does, but that the very nature of God loves through me; just as He put up with the things in me which were not of Him, so He puts up with the things which are not of Him in others through me, and what is manifested is the love of God, the love that suffers long and is kind, the love that does not take account of evil, the love that never fails.

THOUGHTS TO CONSIDER

Has it occurred to you that if the Holy Spirit is living in you, you can love others the same way God loves you?

Are you willing to let the Holy Spirit love others through you?

Have you made it your goal to imitate God and walk in love?

Do you understand that love can only be expressed by actions?

Do you understand that 1 Corinthians 13 describes love by showing us the actions of love?

Jesus Christ showed us His love by giving —

> *He gave up His heavenly home.*
> *He gave up His rights to benefit Himself.*
> *He gave up His life.*

> > *He was given back His heavenly home.*
> > *He was given back all His rights as God.*
> > *He was given back His life.*

> > > *He humbled Himself,*
> > > *therefore He was exalted.*

SCRIPTURES TO KNOW

EPHESIANS 5:1-2
Therefore be imitators of God, as beloved children; and walk in love, just as Christ also loved you, and gave Himself up for us, an offering and a sacrifice to God as a fragrant aroma.

1 JOHN 4:7-11
Beloved, let us love one another, for love is from God; and every one who loves is born of God and knows God. The one who does not love does not know God, for God is love.

By this the love of God was manifested in us, that God has sent His only begotten Son into the world so that we might live through Him. In this is love, not that we loved God, but that He loved us and sent His Son to be the propitiation for our sins.

Beloved, if God so loved us, we also ought to love one another.

EPHESIANS 4:1-2
I, therefore, the prisoner of the Lord, entreat you to walk in a manner worthy of the calling with which you have been called, with all humility and gentleness [meekness], with patience, showing forbearance to one another in love....

1 PETER 5:6
Humble yourselves, therefore, under the mighty hand of God, that He may exalt you at the proper time, casting all your anxiety upon Him, because He cares for you.

HIS
PERSONALITY
&
MINE

Wherefore, accept one another, just as Christ
also accepted us to the glory of God
ROMANS 15:7

As I WALKED BACK toward the house I could see the old-fashioned stool in the front doorway. On the stool was a pint of my favorite kind of ice cream, with a spoon stuck in the top. One of Chuck's gifts to "help my depression"!

I keep telling him that because it has so many calories it CAUSES depression, but he keeps leaving me these little surprises. It made me laugh.

Another time, about 3 A.M., I got up to go to the bathroom. When I came back to bed, it was completely made, and Chuck was hiding in the closet. It made me laugh.

As long as we've been married, Chuck has had to play when we make the bed together. It used to be with our dogs between the covers, or him trying to make it faster than I can. Something to make fun and make me laugh.

We learned that men are more one-dimensional than women — that is, they usually can't concentrate on two things at once, like watch a football game and talk, or read the newspaper and hear their mate talking to them. Chuck decided he would test me to see if I really could do two things at once. I was reading the morning paper and he stood behind me and said very softly, "I'll give you one million dollars for you to buy groceries." I said, "I'll take it!" Of course he was kidding about the amount, but I've never let him forget his word to me. I'm still waiting for the million-dollar budget for my grocery shopping.

Chuck, as I've said, is an idea person. His mind never quits working. When he asked me to marry him he said, "I've been thinking — we could get married after I get out of the army in two years." I told him I thought that would be a good idea. A couple of months later he said, "I've been thinking — we could get married during spring vacation." I thought that was an even better idea! Sometime later he said, "I've been thinking — we could get married between semesters." I was thrilled with that idea. My mother said he couldn't come up with any more ideas about the wedding date, so he quit thinking about that. I didn't know that for the rest of our lives he would be beginning sentences with, "I've been thinking..."

When we had been married twenty-five years, Chuck and I took a temperament analysis test. Chuck tested out impulsive and light-hearted. When I saw the impulsive score I exclaimed, "It fits!" Most impulsive people are also idea people, and Chuck always comes up with something new.

Many times I would never think to do what he is planning. However, once he talks about it with me and I become convinced it is what we should do, I am wholeheartedly behind it.

One problem, however: In about two or three weeks — or maybe two or three months; I never know which — he comes up with what he thinks is a better idea, but it negates the one we are already working on. Chuck feels that I never want him to change his mind. I think that he never sticks with things; if I put my weight down and commit myself, and he changes his mind, I feel adrift. By the way, "impulsive" means changeable.

Of course, in the temperament analysis test I tested out disciplined. I don't like changes or surprises. I like to have time to plan and think. I find it hard to make decisions, while he likes to make snap decisions. I believe this is our hardest area to deal with. When we decide to go in a certain direction and we've both agreed, I feel like I am standing on bedrock. But when he changes his mind, my bedrock turns to quicksand. To be honest, we haven't arrived at a solution to this problem, other than to accept one another, and "beware."

From this temperament test we also discovered that Chuck is subjective while I am objective. Subjective people tend to make emotional decisions, while objective people tend to reason things out to their logical conclusion. Chuck sees the end result — the finished product or goal — while I see all the details required for getting there. He thinks I'm a balloon-popper, while I think he doesn't count the cost. Both of us believe we are right, and there is often a struggle giving up our right to be right.

I like to have small gatherings at our home so we can sit around the table and visit deeply. Chuck likes to have large groups so we don't have to visit deeply. And besides, he doesn't just want to sit around and visit; he wants to be playing pickle ball or pitching horseshoes. He wants to be DOING something.

Chuck has a choleric personality. I have named him President of the World because he likes to be in charge, have control, and make decisions. Many times cholerics are impatient and want things done immediately.

I have a phlegmatic personality. People like me are more laid back, and are more content with the way things are.

But Chuck and I are both dominant. That means we both have opinions and we think those opinions are right. By "dominant" I don't mean "dominating," but rather "confident" and "assertive." I tell him that since I'm more laid back, I've done the most adjusting because otherwise I would not have done half of the things he's talked me into. He is not convinced.

It has taken years to understand and work out these differences. Our greatest help has come from the Bible. We are told to accept one another just as God has accepted us in Christ Jesus (Romans 15:7). We are told to have unity (Ephesians 4:3). We are told to walk in love, trying to learn how to please the Lord (Ephesians 5:2,10). We are told not to think more highly of ourselves than we ought to think (Romans 12:3). We are told to serve one another (Galatians 5:13). We are told to give a blessing — to do something kind or say something nice — in order to receive a blessing (1 Peter 3:9).

Chuck and I respond to one another best when we can talk things over and understand one another. We noticed that other couples don't seem to talk as much as we do. Then friends of ours sent us a tape by Dr. Gary Chapman, associate pastor of Calvary Baptist Church in Winston-Salem, North Carolina. He has written a book called *Toward a Growing Marriage.* On that tape he tells us that there are five different kinds of love languages. These five ways are how we act out love to one another, or how we feel loved if it is done for us.

I think I have all five, but really I think he means we probably have one predominant one. The five are: *words, time, touch, service,* and *gifts.*

I believe Chuck and I both have the same love language, and it is words. Kind words. Talking things over, talking things out, talking for fun, talking about feelings. Sharing our lives with each other. I'm not talking about how MUCH one talks, but what KIND of talk there is. I'm speaking of quality rather than quantity. When a job is well done, a person with the love language of words needs feedback, either spoken or written, that tells him how he did. A person with this love language feels loved when the words are positive and supportive. Unkind words will dishearten a person who shows love with kindness. Unkind words may cause a person with this kind of love language to want to give up.

The love language of time can also include talking, but sometimes it means just being there. Many people like to have you watch TV with them even when you don't talk — such as men who are watching a ball game that the wife is not inter- ested in, but if she just sits there and knits and is with him, he is happy. The trouble can come when her love language is words, while his is just time and he needs no words.

Do you know anyone who is always touching you — taking your hand, or putting an arm around you, hugs and kisses, just being close? When Chuck and I first got our king- size bed (after having a double-size bed during our first twenty-two years of marriage), I was lonely and didn't know why. Something was missing and I just couldn't figure out what. It took me a couple of years to understand that I just needed to be touched more. In our narrower double bed, touching one another more had been inevitable.

We have some young friends who are doing well in their marriage. He compliments her all the time, buys her gifts often, and just thinks the world of her. She said to me one day, "If he would only help me more around the house! He makes such messes, and then when company comes I have to clean up what I just cleaned up ten minutes before." I asked her if she thought her love language was service. We think it probably is. She feels loved when he helps her out around the house, and when he does projects for her that SHE thinks are important. He feels he's showing her love by all the gifts he buys for her. I have another friend who gives me and others gifts all the time. She is so thoughtful. This is the way she shows her love.

It's interesting that the way we show love is usually the way we feel loved when it is done for us.

Even our children respond differently. One can be corrected with gentle words, while another child needs physical discipline. One responds well when doing things together, while another is a loner. One may seem to hang on you all the time, while another doesn't even want to be touched. One is always picking flowers and making drawings to give you, while another wants you to wait on him hand and foot.

When we discovered that our love language is kind words, we could see how much we needed to guard our tongues and provide the atmosphere that will make us both feel loved. Because God tells us in Galatians 5:13, "By love serve one another," we must do it. The message that keeps coming to my mind over and over again as I write this book is the importance of doing what God says. And, of course, that is called obedience. It is also called righteousness, doing what is right according to God's instructions.

In Mark 8:34-35, Jesus says,

> If anyone wishes to come after Me, let him deny himself, and take up his cross and follow Me. For whoever wishes to save his life shall lose it; and whoever loses his life for My sake and the gospel's shall save it.

The thought of denying myself is hard, but it helped when I found out the Greek tense for this Scripture. The phrase "wishes to come" is aorist active, which means it's a fact you wish to come, and you alone do this action. "Deny" is aorist middle, which means at the point of denying yourself the Lord steps in and helps you do the denying. So, at the point of obedience the Lord helps us to obey.

So many times we want our own way and spend time being upset because we are not getting it. We don't make eye contact, we don't talk, or if we do there is no sparkle in our voice. We mope around and act sad. We don't even realize that sadness is just another expression of anger. We often turn anger into sadness.

Not long ago Chuck and I went away for the weekend. When we arrived at the hotel we had a disagreement about where to park the car. I know this sounds silly, but that's what happened. I thought, *What a terrible way to start off our weekend together,* so I said something funny and took his hand and pretended we had never had the disagreement. Later, hoping I could get some more insights into how to write this book, I asked Chuck to tell me what else I did for him that made him happy. He said, "I like it when you say something light and happy to break the tension after we've had a disagreement."

I want to tell you that I didn't feel like being obedient, but when I did obey, the Lord stepped in and helped me. I also think he helped Chuck to respond lovingly too. I believe when I am obedient I set up circumstances that allow Chuck to choose for obedience too. When one is disobedient it gives an excuse for the other to do the same. But when the right path is chosen, obedience for your mate is made easier. Even though obedience is hard sometimes, we have to look ahead and count the cost if we choose our own way. We must not be shortsighted. We should keep asking ourselves what the end result will be if we choose to act independently of God. He has already told us that if we lose our life for His sake, we will save it.

The Lord also says in Matthew 7 that to hear His words and act upon them is like being a wise man who built his house upon the rock; and the rains and floods came, and the winds blew, and yet the house did not fall; for it had been founded upon the rock. When we do as we're told, we are building our lives on the Rock, the Lord Jesus Christ (1 Corinthians 10:4). The Rock is solid footing; the Rock is tried and tested; the Rock is trustworthy, not changeable; and the Rock is very wise. Psalm 18:31-32 says it best:

> For who is God, but the LORD?
> And who is a rock, except our God,
> The God who girds me with strength,
> And makes my way blameless?

When our way is blameless we have God's blessing. To be blessed is to have a sense of God's approval. Sometimes it is translated "happy." It is being in circumstances that you would never choose and do not even like, and yet you are responding the way God instructs you. Therefore you have a sense of His approval. Ultimately His approval is what we should be striving for, for His ways bring peace to our hearts.

Shortly after I received the contract for this book, Chuck and I were driving home. I was feeling so "in love" with him. I told him so. He said with a smile, "You're just saying that because you're writing that book!" Soon after I made him oat-bran pancakes for breakfast. Again he said, "You're just doing that because you're writing that book." Then we were at a booksellers convention staying in a lovely hotel. When I got up in the middle of the night, I saw that Chuck had actually put the toilet seat down. I thought, *He's just doing that because I'm writing that book!*

It's been fun. I tell him I'm not going to finish writing this book for the rest of our lives, so he'll have to continue being nice to me. He doesn't know what I'm going to write about him, and he's worried.

Chuck shares himself so openly with others that I'm not afraid to share about us either. (By the way, Chuck is going to edit this book and everything in it will be by his permission.) However, when we were young I can remember him telling one of our teachers that he would never tell others anything about problems he might have. For someone who was so determined to be closed rather than open, he sure has changed.

The reason he has changed, however, is because God changed him. Chuck discovered that he could help more people by being vulnerable than he could by looking strong and problem-free. He learned from 2 Corinthians 1:3-5 that God wants us to comfort others with the same comfort we have received from Him during our troubles.

On the other hand, my problem over the years has been saying too much. I've had to learn to keep quiet and keep more things to myself. (In the next chapter I'll tell you why.)

I see Chuck as being opinionated yet teachable, quiet yet talkative, goal-oriented yet sensitive, hating conflict yet allowing conflict to come to resolve, fun yet serious, persevering yet changeable, loving, gentle, kind, godly. He is a mixture of so many things. Assured, yet insecure. He is a human being who loves to tease, to have fun, to work hard, and to accomplish goals. He is a balanced man.

This balance did not happen overnight. It comes from doing things right and doing things wrong. Then we think about it and weigh in our minds the outcome: When I did *this,* then *that* happened, and when I did *that, this* happened. When I was disobedient, I made a mess of things. When I obeyed, the Lord worked things out for me. Which, then, am I going to choose: to be obedient, or disobedient?

We are to think over what has happened, and draw conclusions. Then we decide which way is the best to go: our way, or God's way.

Jeremiah 17:5-8 tells us the way God would do it:

Thus says the LORD,
"Cursed is the man who trusts in mankind
And makes flesh his strength,
And whose heart turns away from the LORD.

"For he will be like a bush in the desert
And will not see when prosperity comes,
But will live in stony wastes in the wilderness,
A land of salt without inhabitant.

"Blessed is the man who trusts in the LORD
And whose trust is the LORD.

"For he will be like a tree planted by the water,
that extends its roots by a stream
And will not fear when the heat comes;
But its leaves will be green,
And it will not be anxious in a year of drought
Nor cease to yield fruit."

When we are angry with our mates, the first thing we do is run to someone to tell them how we hurt. I used to talk to Chuck's mother. She was always a good listener. However, when she thought I had said enough she would tell me, "You LOVE my boy." I received good advice from her, but God says not to run to mankind — not to make mankind our strength.

I can always get someone to be on my side when telling a story: Add a little here and leave out a little there, and I can slant anything to make myself look good. But the Lord is the one who searches the heart and tests the mind. He is the one who will give to each man according to his ways, according to the results of his deeds (Revelation 2:23, 1 Chronicles 28:9).

When I think of my life and my ways, I don't want to be like a bush in the desert with no root to hold it secure. This bush is like a tumbleweed. I don't want to be tossed around and back and forth because I've listened to someone's advice and taken it, and it didn't work. God says that brings a curse. God says HE is the Wonderful Counselor. When we talk with someone, we need to make sure that person's advice matches up with the Word of God.

I want to be blessed by the Lord. I want to be like that tree planted by the water. I want my roots to go deep so that I don't have to worry when the heat comes and there is drought. (Those times when you don't "feel love" are your times of drought.) I want to keep my leaves green so that I'll never have to worry about not yielding fruit. I want to keep on producing the fruit of kindness, and love, and gentleness, and patience. I want to keep on producing no matter how I feel. I want to trust in the Lord and order my life for Him, so that blessing will come. I want to bring honor and glory to His name.

When we are obedient, and all turns out for our good (even though at times we think it is bad), it brings glory to

God. The reason? We trust Him. We do what He says, and prove that His will is good and acceptable and perfect (Romans 12:2).

God is not our adversary. He is on our side. He wants the best for us. For some reason we think that He is trying to ruin our fun. But just the opposite is true. He has given us parameters to live within to protect us so we CAN have fun — so we'll have peace and happiness.

> And the work of righteousness will be peace,
> And the service of righteousness,
>> quietness and confidence forever. (Isaiah 32:17)

Our job is to do what is right. God takes care of the rest.

To have peace is the greatest thing, and God says we will have it as we do what is right. What do we have when we mess up? We have unrest, confusion, and broken relationships — just the opposite of peace.

Why not choose peace?

THOUGHTS TO CONSIDER

Do you know the temperament traits of your mate?

Have you studied your mate so you know his likes and dislikes?

What do you do for your husband that he likes best?

Do you know his love-language?

Have you told the Lord you will accept your mate just as he is, and not try to change him?

Have you decided to deny yourself and keep on following the Lord by loving your mate the way the Lord wants you to love?

SCRIPTURES TO KNOW

MARK 8:34-35
And He summoned the multitude with His disciples, and said to them, "If any wishes to come after Me, let him deny himself, and take up his cross and follow Me. For whoever wishes to save his life shall lose it; and whoever loses his life for My sake and the gospel's shall save it."

2 SAMUEL 22:2-3
The LORD is my rock and my fortress and my deliverer;
My God, my rock, in whom I take refuge;
My shield and the horn of my salvation,
My stronghold and my refuge.

HIS COMMUNICATION & MINE

Let no unwholesome word proceed from your mouth,
but only such a word as is good for edification
according to the need of the moment,
that it may give grace to those who hear....
And be kind to one another, tender-hearted,
forgiving each other, just as God in Christ
also has forgiven you.

EPHESIANS 4:29,32

I WAS INITIALLY ATTRACTED to Chuck because he has a gentle and quiet spirit. He is a good listener and I like to be heard. He made me feel that what I said was important to him. He was attracted to me because I am outgoing and talkative. No one is a stranger to me. Both of us have qualities that we admired in each other and did not have ourselves.

But what we admired so much about each other before marriage soon became our greatest irritation afterward. He thought I talked to too many people and too much. I wished he could be more outgoing and not so quiet. When we had disagreements, I wanted to talk about them "right now," and he "never" wanted to talk about them. I wanted to talk so we could FIND peace. He did *not* want to talk so we could KEEP peace. Both of us had good motives, but we didn't approach our problems the same way, nor did we understand each other.

Chuck wanted to keep peace so badly that he did not tell me how my interrupting was driving him crazy. He told me this only after we had been married for eleven years. When we had a disagreement I wanted to make peace so much that I just kept pursuing him, trying to make him talk. But he wanted to keep the peace so much that he wouldn't talk. He was driving me crazy! I was driving him crazy!

We did not know the terms *expressive* and *nonexpressive*. We knew about introverts and extroverts and that we fit those descriptions, but Chuck had no idea that I NEEDED to talk about my feelings, and I had no idea that he didn't even KNOW what his feelings were until he had time to think about them. Initially when we disagreed the only feeling he could express was anger.

And then, I saw a contradiction in him too. Sometimes he would talk and talk and talk. At other times he would just sit there; his body was present, but he was nowhere around. Many times after going out for coffee with our friends they would ask me later if Chuck was all right. I would say, "Oh, he's just tired" or "He had a busy week," or "He's got a lot on his mind," and on and on.

I didn't know then that Chuck was goal-oriented, and so when he was counseling or had a goal to talk about, he would and could talk as much as I could. But he has trouble with "small talk" — visiting with people without having a goal in mind.

Once we stayed with my parents during the Christmas holidays. Before we drove back across the mountains to Seattle, we took Mom and Dad out for dinner, and then to visit with my brother and his family one last time. During dinner Chuck barely spoke. He just ate, and sat there. I was being Miss Bubbly, trying to keep the conversation going. I knew he wanted to go when he started tapping his fingers on the table. When we later stopped at my brother's home, Chuck would not sit down. He walked from one room to another and then back again. He leaned against the doorway. He wandered away again. He was using body language to tell me he wanted to leave. He had been visiting far too long for his comfort, but didn't know how to tell me straight out that he had a goal — to get home.

Dr. James Dobson on his *Focus on the Family* radio program once told how Shirley, his wife, had to teach him about herself. But she taught him in a nonthreatening way so he could receive it. I don't know how nonthreatening I was; in fact, I'm sure I overdid it when I told Chuck I did not want him to communicate ONLY by his body language any more; I said I wanted him to talk to me, to reason, and then we could come to a mutual decision.

When I said those things, Chuck didn't even know what he had been doing. As we wrote in our book *Incompatibility: Grounds for a Great Marriage,* body language accounts for 55 percent of communication; tone of voice is 35%, intuition 2%, and words only 8%. The poor man! Now when we are out for coffee with friends and Chuck stretches, someone will usually ask, "Is it time to go home?" He doesn't have any secrets any more.

In the last chapter we discussed doing for others what you would have them do for you. When Chuck and I realized we were so different in our need for visiting, we had to act on what we had learned. When church is over, I like to stand around and visit. Chuck likes to go immediately to the car. He used to slip out, and I would find myself looking for him because I didn't know where he was. We compromised: Now he tells me when he leaves, and says I can visit as long as I want. Our friends know where he is, and go out to the car where he is listening to tapes, or reading. Somehow he feels more comfortable sitting in the car than standing around "free" in the church.

When we go to weddings or anniversary receptions, Chuck now visits and looks happy doing it. He has told me not to misread his happy look, and not to assume he is having a wonderful time. We have compromised: He now visits more than he would normally, and I visit less.

And yet, as I said, if he has a goal he talks a lot. When we are out with a couple counseling, I can't get a word in edgewise — or at least it seems that way. We've had to talk about that too, and not be upset if we step on each other's lines. After all, we neither one would purposely hurt the other.

The key to our communication is to understand how each of us do it. He has to think about things for quite a while before he knows how he feels. I know almost immediately how I feel. I have to give him time to think. He has to give me hope that he WILL think, and we WILL talk at some future time.

We differ because he is a peacekeeper and I am a peacemaker. He thinks if he doesn't talk about a problem it will go away, but I believe it will get bigger. Chuck says that communication during conflict is like vomiting: He hates to get to it, but he does feel better when it's over! Before we understood this principle he used to tell me that I liked conflict. Now we know I just want to get back in fellowship again.

Peacekeepers want to keep everything smooth and peaceful. They think that the problem will go away if it is never mentioned. Peacemakers want to talk about it and make peace right away. It looks like peacemakers are causing a big conflict (especially to the nonexpressive one), but by talking it out and finding out the underlying problem, they are making peace.

The peacekeeper usually says something like this: "Why on earth are we going over this again? I thought we had already discussed it. We just say the same things over again." But the peacemaker wants to talk it over again because he or she thinks, "If I can just say it one more time another way, I'll be understood." Like so many others, Chuck and I were going over the same ground again and again, so we had to learn HOW to solve conflict.

Our first insight into settling conflict came when I studied the Sermon on the Mount in another Precept Bible Study. In Matthew 5, this sermon opens with Jesus giving eight characteristics (the "Beatitudes") of a true Christian:

> Blessed are the poor in spirit...
> Blessed are those who mourn...
> Blessed are those who hunger and thirst for righteousness...
> Blessed are the merciful...
> Blessed are the pure in heart...
> Blessed are the peacemakers...
> Blessed are those who have been persecuted for the sake of
>   righteousness.... Blessed are you when men revile you,
>   and persecute you, and say all kinds of evil against you
>   falsely, on account of Me.

I believe the first four Beatitudes match up with the last four like this:

When we are poor in spirit, we see there is nothing in us

apart from Jesus Christ that makes us worthy, and it is only BY HIM that we can be saved and live a consistent, Christlike life. Because we understand this, we can be more understanding of the faults of others and be merciful to them. We know it is only by the grace of God that He loves us; therefore, if He loved us while we were unlovable, we can be merciful and love others the same way.

When we mourn over sin we become pure in heart, because our mourning over sin causes us to stop sinning and to seek righteousness. We are unable to help ourselves (being poor in spirit) and we understand when we acted our own way that the result was sin. When we mourn over sin and are repentant, God gives us a pure heart. A pure heart is a heart whose motives are unmixed with evil intent. This kind of heart is completely and totally single-minded toward doing what God wants. A person with a pure heart wants everything in his life to measure up to God's standards.

When we are meek we have God's power in our life to accept what comes into our life as coming from the hand of God. And, as my friend Kay Arthur teaches, we know all things have been filtered through fingers of love. Since we realize that God is in complete control of our lives, even over what people say to us, we can be peacemakers. We are not afraid of what will happen to us when we try to be a peacemaker because we trust completely that He is in control of all situations. We are trusting so much in the Lord that we do not think of ourselves at all, but only about what He wants.

Because we've put our trust completely in the Lord, we hunger and thirst for righteousness. We want to know exactly what He says in His Word for us to do. When we are righteous, our fellowship with the Lord will satisfy us beyond measure. However, men will persecute us and revile us, and say all kinds of evil against us falsely, because we are following the Lord so completely. But the Lord says we are blessed when this happens.

Another reason people make fun of us and treat us badly is because we've removed their excuse to sin. In John 15, Jesus tells us about this:

> This I command you, that you love one another. If [and it's true] the world hates you, you know that it has hated Me before it hated you. If [and it's true] you were of the world, the world would love its own; but because you are not of the world, but I chose you out of the world, therefore the world hates you.
>
> Remember the word that I said to you, "A slave is not greater than his master." If [and it's true] they persecuted Me, they will also persecute you. If [and it's true] they kept My word, they will keep yours also.
>
> But all these things they will do to you for My name's sake, because they do not know the One who sent Me. If I had not spoken to them, they would not have sin, *but now they have no excuse for their sin.*

People may accuse you of having a "holier than thou" attitude because you won't join in their activities. Or they may exclude you from their conversations or plans. It may not be anything other than the Lord in you causing them to feel uncomfortable, and so they do not want to be around you. Just remember, though: The Lord tells us that we are blessed when this happens to us.

Here are other principles we had to discover about communication:

We learned that our heart-attitude must be right in regard to each other. Proverbs 18:12 reads:

> Before destruction the heart of man is haughty,
> But humility goes before honor.

We had to learn how powerful is the tongue..

> Death and life are in the power of the tongue,
> And those who love it will eat its fruit. (Proverbs 18:21)

We had to pray for our tongues to be controlled.

> Set a guard, O LORD, over my mouth;
> Keep watch over the door of my lips. (Psalm 141:3)

I had to learn to listen.

> He who gives an answer before he hears,
> It is folly and shame to him. (Proverbs 18:13)

Chuck had to learn to ask questions and not presume.

> Through presumption comes nothing but strife,
> But with those who receive counsel is wisdom.
> (Proverbs 13:10)

Both of us had to realize how sensitive we are.

> The spirit of a man can endure his sickness,
> But a broken spirit who can bear? (Proverbs 18:14)

We had to learn to respond, not react.

> A gentle answer turns away wrath,
> But a harsh word stirs up anger.
>
> The tongue of the wise makes knowledge acceptable,
> But the mouth of fools spouts folly.
>
> The eyes of the LORD are in every place,
> watching the evil and the good.
>
> A soothing tongue is a tree of life,
> But perversion in it crushes the spirit. (Proverbs 15:1-4)

We had to listen to reproof and to discipline ourselves.

> He who neglects discipline despises himself,
> But he who listens to reproof acquires understanding.
>
> The fear of the LORD is the instruction for wisdom,
> And before honor comes humility. (Proverbs 15:32-33)

We learned we must not have a critical spirit.

> The heart of the righteous ponders how to answer,
> But the mouth of the wicked pours out evil things.
> (Proverbs 15:28)

We learned that we needed to be slow to anger.

> But let everyone be quick to hear, slow to speak and
> slow to anger; for the anger of man does not achieve the
> righteousness of God. (James 1:19-20)

We learned how Christ responded to suffering; how He let His wounds heal us. In other words, He allowed Himself to be wounded so we could be healed. By responding as Christ did, we can help heal others too.

For you have been called for this purpose, since Christ also suffered for you, leaving you an example that you should follow in His steps, "who committed no sin, nor was any deceit found in His mouth"; and while being reviled, He did not revile in return; while suffering, He uttered no threats, but kept entrusting Himself to Him who judges righteously; and He Himself bore our sins in His body on the cross, that we might die to sin and live to righteousness; for by His wounds you were healed. (1 Peter 2:21-24)

We learned what improves communication.

Let no unwholesome [rotten] word proceed from your mouth, but only such a word as is good for edification [building up one another] according to the need of the moment, that it may give grace to those who hear. And do not grieve the Holy Spirit of God, by whom you were sealed for the day of redemption. Let all bitterness and wrath and anger and clamor and slander be put away from you, along with all malice. And be kind to one another, tender-hearted, forgiving each other, just as God in Christ also has forgiven you. (Ephesians 4:29-32)

And so, as those who have been chosen of God, holy and beloved, put on a heart of compassion, kindness, humility, gentleness [meekness] and patience; bearing with one another, and forgiving each other, whoever has a complaint against any one; just as the Lord forgave you, so also should you. And beyond all these things put on love, which is the perfect bond of unity. (Colossians 3:12-14)

Let your speech always be with grace, seasoned, as it were, with salt, so that you may know how you should respond to each person. (Colossians 4:6)

To sum up, let all be harmonious, sympathetic, brotherly, kind-hearted, and humble in spirit; not returning evil for evil, or insult for insult, but giving a blessing instead; for you were called for the very purpose that you might inherit [claim as your own] a blessing. (1 Peter 3:8-9)

We learned what God commands us if we want to love our life with one another and enjoy good days.

For "Let him who means to love life and see good days refrain his tongue from evil and his lips from speaking guile [saying one thing and meaning another], and let him turn away from evil and do good; let him seek peace and pursue it. For the eyes of the Lord are upon the righteous, and his ears attend to their prayer, but the face of the Lord is against those who do evil." (1 Peter 3:10-12)

Our communication improved as a direct result of learning these principles. It was work — hard work — but worth it.

We have learned to do what is called "quick listening." The term is taken from James 1:19 — "But let everyone be quick to hear, slow to speak and slow to anger." Here's how quick listening works:

I let Chuck tell me everything he feels, WITHOUT INTER-

RUPTING HIM. He has no need to get angry, for I let him speak. Then I repeat back to Chuck what he said, and if I get it wrong he can correct me until I get it right.

Then we reverse the roles and I tell him how I feel about the problem or disagreement, without him interrupting me. Then he repeats back what I said. When we both have our feelings out, we proceed to talk back and forth normally.

Before we learned how to do this I would evaluate everything Chuck said before he could make all his points. When we learned about quick listening, we had been told to keep our feeling sentences short so our partner can easily repeat back to us what we are saying. Chuck went first, and he talked and talked and talked. I said, "You're talking too long. I can't remember everything you're getting wrong!" He smiled, handed me pen and paper, and said, "Here, take notes." So...Chuck changed the rules. We do not repeat back one another's short sentences, but instead must listen until the other is completely finished. It's hard to keep quiet till he's through, but that's the rule.

Quick listening has helped us so much. Chuck does not feel attacked because I don't have to keep pursuing him, and I do not feel punished because he refuses to talk. He can express his thoughts in order and does not forget what he is about to say. And because I don't keep interrupting him like I used to, he keeps talking. Using quick listening makes us both winners.

In this way we do not grieve the Holy Spirit. To grieve the Holy Spirit is to do what you know you aren't supposed to do. It is an active thing. It is bursting out with angry words when you know the Lord has told you to keep your mouth shut. The expressive person is often guilty of this. On the other hand, to *quench* the Holy Spirit is when you do NOT do what you know He is telling you, such as talking with your mate.

Quenching is a passive thing. No one knows what is going on inside of you, or that the Holy Spirit is telling you to communicate something.

A nonexpressive looks good no matter what, for he or she can remain calm and gentle even while screaming inside. An expressive often looks out of control because by comparison he or she is talking a lot. That's why Chuck couldn't stand to hear my voice get tighter and higher when we were having a disagreement.

It's a very subtle thing, but nonexpressives are often angrier than anyone would believe, even themselves. Today in the newspaper a baseball player is reported to have bad-mouthed his owner. Afterward he exclaimed he did not know where it had come from. The player said he normally kept quiet, but he had had this in his heart for a long time, and somehow it just came out. Jesus says in Matthew 12:34, "For the mouth speaks out of that which fills the heart." When the Bible speaks of the "heart" it is interchangeable with the "mind." So...we must be careful, as we've already seen, what our mind dwells on.

You need to know if you have an expressive or nonexpressive mate so you can communicate in the way your mate needs. Does he tell you he doesn't know why he is angry? Believe him, and give him more time to get in touch with his feelings. Does he tell you everything that is on his mind, and tell you to listen and respond without walking away? If you can't respond now, you need to promise to talk later, while your partner needs to back off and give you time to think.

Either way, each must teach the other in a nonthreatening way how they need to communicate. Tell one another how much better you could communicate if you could both identify how you typically react in a conflict. Do you withdraw, or do you pursue? Are you nonexpressive, or expressive?

When Chuck and I married we decided we would never cut each other down. We do not practice sarcasm. Proverbs 12:18 says, "There is one who speaks rashly like the thrusts of a sword, but the tongue of the wise brings healing. I think this proverbs is talking about sarcasm. Words that "thrust at you like a sword" can be funny when everyone is feeling good, but sometimes when one is not in a good mood he ends up worrying about "what they *really* meant by that."

There ARE times when Chuck or I feel cut down, because the other one does not agree with our way of thinking. However, that is not the same as purposely trying to put down the other person.

Many times Chuck and I have stayed up late trying to resolve a disagreement because we did not want to go against the verse, "Do not let the sun go down on your anger." We were sincere, but I don't believe we were correct in our understanding of these words in Ephesians 4:26. I believe most of us misinterpret this verse, and therefore carry a heavy load that was never intended for us.

My understanding is that the Greek word used in this verse for anger means "impulse." In *Vine's Expository Dictionary* this word is defined as "a more settled or abiding condition of the mind, frequently with a view to taking revenge." So the kind of anger we must not keep overnight is that state of mind where we are planning revenge.

Webster's gives the word *impulse* this definition: "An excitement to action arising from a state of mind or some stimulus; a sudden inclination to act without conscious thought; a motive or tendency coming from within." I believe we can still feel the emotion of what we call anger, hurt, or frustration, and we can feel it until the next day, but we must not have the kind of anger that has us making plans to get even. Our goal in life should be to settle our differences as soon as possible, and we should be working toward that goal all the time. But it is not always possible to get rid of feelings before the sun goes down. I believe, however, that it is imperative to let your partner know that your love for each other is first and foremost, and that you WILL work it out.

Chuck and I have made it a part of our lives to reach out and touch each other before going to sleep on nights when we have a disagreement that has not been resolved. This is our way of telling each other that we are completely committed to working out our differences. It gives us peace as we go to sleep. We may not have a compromise or resolution YET, but we pledge to talk tomorrow or the next day.

And then, too, we want to be obedient because God has told us in Ephesians 4:31 to be kind, tenderhearted, forgiving one another as God in Christ Jesus has forgiven us. That's another reason for the touching at bedtime. Sometimes we tap each other three times — meaning "I...love...you."

It seems that most things we've learned have been learned the hard way. We often do it wrong and experience the consequences before we are willing to try the right way and see that it works. Many times I've thought how much smarter it would be to do it the Lord's way first; then we wouldn't have to go through all the misery.

Someone told me that there are five levels in the learning process: rote, recognition, restating, relational, and realization, and all five apply to spiritual learning.

Let's say we are trying to learn a principle from the Bible. When we know something by rote it is only by memory with no real understanding. It is the kind of learning we did when we crammed for tests in school. This learning can be repeated back but reasoning or logic is not there. This is the stage in which we say, "Our pastor says…" or "Chuck says…" or "Charles Swindoll says…" or "Kay Arthur says…."

Recognition is that stage in learning when we hear the principle again and say to ourselves, "Oh, I know that; this is familiar, I've heard it before." For some, this is as far as Bible learning ever goes. Chuck and I have taught people who say they "know" what we are talking about, but the way they conduct their lives gives evidence for just the opposite. Just to recognize a certain principle doesn't mean we "know" it. If we "knew" it, we'd practice it. However, this is where we can be the mt dangerous because "we do not know that we do not know."

The third stage of learning is being able to restate the material. We can paraphrase it and use it in conversation. Yet we still do not *know* very much about it. This is the transition level, however, from no understanding to understanding. Thinking begins here.

Relational learning and thinking means making connections between one thing and another. It is seeing the relationship between a principle, an action, and the result of that action. It is seeing the connection between two passages of Scripture, such as Romans 8:28, where God says that "all things work together for good to those who love God, to those who are called according to His purpose," and the story of Joseph in Genesis. Joseph was sold by his brothers and taken to Egypt as a slave, but later was appointed by Pharaoh to rule over Egypt, and no one could do anything in all the land of Egypt without Joseph's permission (Genesis 41-44). When there was a famine, Joseph's brothers came to buy food from him, not knowing he was their brother. When Joseph revealed himself, he comforted them and told them,

And do not be grieved or angry with yourselves, because you sold me here; for God sent me before you to preserve life. For the famine has been in the land these two years, and there are still five years in which there will be neither plowing nor harvesting. And God sent me before you to preserve for you a remnant in the earth, and to keep you alive by a great deliverance. *Now, therefore, it was not you who sent me here, but God;* and He has made me a father to Pharaoh and lord of all his household and ruler over all the land of Egypt. (Genesis 45:5-8)

Humanly speaking, everything looked hopeless for Joseph, and it's often the same in our lives. We don't know how to work things out ourselves, but we do know that God is working despite our ignorance. To learn on the relational level, our thinking would be like this: "If God could and did work through Joseph's life, and He says He will do the same for me...then I'll trust Him." Another thought could be, "How did Joseph go through his trials? What were his trials and what was his attitude? We see that he went through them trusting in God, and even though he went from a slave to a high position, then to prison unjustly accused, then back to a higher position — yet he did it all with the right attitude. He kept entrusting himself to God and waiting for His rescue.

The final learning stage, realization, is coming to understand fully what God has been trying to tell us. Full realization comes AFTER we have acted on the principles we have been learning, AFTER we've decided to be obedient. We decide to conduct our lives according to God's principles, and when His principles work we say, "Oh, now I see why I had to respond that way; now I know why I had to do that. I see. I understand."

When we come to full realization we can see how the passage fits with other Scripture. It impacts our lives when we live it out. After incorporating it into our daily living, it becomes "us." We realize and understand what God was trying to tell us all along. And when we get to this point of understanding, it makes one wonder why others can't see it.

Let me give you an example of this learning process. It's not from Scripture, but from our lives. I like to keep a basket of unshelled peanuts on the coffee table in our family room. Many mornings I noticed that Chuck sure was messy with the peanut shells, and I wished he wouldn't drop so many on the rug. I mentioned to Chuck how messy he was, but he denied it. Each day I observed the same mess again.

One evening Chuck asked me if we had any rat traps. When I asked him why, he said he thought he could see a couple of eyes looking at him from underneath the old organ. "You do not!" I said. "Okay, I don't," he said. We went to investigate. We moved the organ and saw a tail disappear up inside it. We saw rat droppings on the rug. We also saw the relationship between the rat and the mess with the peanut shells. I came to full understanding that it was not Chuck making the mess...it was the rat!

When we are in the rote, recognition, and restating part of the learning process, it's observation. I observed the mess; I recognized it again each day. I still didn't know the truth, for I was sure Chuck was doing it, and I kept restating that to him. Then the relationship between the peanut shells and the rat became apparent when I thought about what I saw behind the organ. Relational learning is the interpretation of the data, while realization is the application of it to our lives.

So it is with learning communication skills from Scripture. It takes knowing them, trying them out to see if they work. And when they do work, we come to full realization that God's ways are best.

This is a lifetime process. We must never stop observing the Scriptures, and during this process we must always keep in mind that Scripture interprets Scripture. Experience is never the determiner of our actions; the Word must be. But with the correct action comes experience. And, as Romans 5:3-5 says,

>...we exult in our tribulations; knowing that tribulation brings about perseverance, and perseverance proven character; and proven character, hope; and hope does not disappoint...

"Proven character" here can also be translated "experience." The experience not only brings proven character — or, in other words, approval from the Lord — but it also gives us hope. This hope means we will never be disappointed in the Lord when we do things His way. I am convinced that God's ways are the right ways.

Recently I lost my temper and proved once again that my ways are not God's ways. To describe what I did honestly is to say that I sinned. I asked Chuck for forgiveness. He forgave me, but we were both miserable for it takes a while to recover. When I woke up the next morning I thought of Psalm 85:10 which says, "Righteousness and peace kiss each other." I hadn't been righteous and I had no peace. In fact, righteousness and peace were not even cuddling.

Chuck and I talked and determined to become friends again. Knowing what I know about peace coming from righteousness, it wasn't worth it to lose my temper. It's much easier to do it right in the beginning.

Even though Chuck and I are different in our ways of communicating, the Lord says we need to accept one another just as He has accepted us. When we do, the other feels special, and when our mate feels special, so do we.

Obedience on my part — on your part — allows God to work in His time, in His way, for His purpose.

THOUGHTS TO CONSIDER

Are you expressive or nonexpressive? What about your mate

Are you a peacekeeper or a peacemaker?

Do you care enough about your relationship with your mate to go through pain in order to have peace? Or are you avoiding pain, and trying to keep peace by staying silent when there is disagreement between you?

Are you willing to learn communication skills so your relationships will grow stronger and more loving?

Are you aware that words can either drain a person of energy or give them energy to go on? (Kind words give grace — unmerited favor — to others.)

Do you want God's ways in your life more than you want your own?

SCRIPTURES TO KNOW

EPHESIANS 4:29-32
Let no unwholesome word proceed from your mouth, but only such a word as is good for edification according to the need of the moment, that it may give grace to those who hear. And do not grieve the Holy Spirit of God, by whom you were sealed for the day of redemption. Let all bitterness and wrath and anger and clamor and slander be put away from you, along with all malice. And be kind to one another, tender-hearted, forgiving each other, just as God in Christ also has forgiven you.

HIS GOALS & MINE

For man does not originate from woman, but woman from man;
for indeed man was not created for the woman's sake,
but woman for the man's sake.... However, in the Lord,
neither is woman independent of man, nor is man
independent of woman. For as the woman originates from the man,
so also the man has his birth through the woman;
and all things originate from God.

1 CORINTHIANS 11:8-9, 11-12

Y ESTERDAY I FOUND a list of "thoughts" I had written
down in 1983. Two things on that list fit this chapter.

The first: "Chuck expands me — my experiences. Thank
him! He pushes me — it's OK."

The other: "Ask God to unlock my heart to understand
Chuck, and his heart to understand me."

God has answered my prayer. Our first book could never
have been written if God had not opened our hearts to understand each other. And we would not have written our book
together if Chuck had not pushed me into it.

Chuck and I have been teaching together for a number of

years now. We've learned new things, and as we have, we have added them to our teaching — new things about us, and new things about the Lord and what He wants us to do. For many years we taught separately; however, in our Sunday school class I was always in the back of the room raising my hand to add some Scripture or comment. We were a team then, too, but we did not stand side by side and teach. The day came when Chuck asked me to help him teach on communication. After we finished that series, Chuck said, "I never want you to sit down again. I want you to teach by my side."

Teaching together is one of the delights of our lives. Chuck is funny, I am more serious. I'll tell you more about our teaching in the chapter "His Gifts and Mine."

I'm writing this book to show how I have learned to stand by Chuck in our marriage, and he by me — side by side, and not one in front of the other. We have not always been side by side. And even when I thought we were, Chuck had it in his mind that if we couldn't agree, *he* would make the final decision. That is not "side by side." Chuck thought he was the deciding factor, and God could work through HIS mistakes in MY life. In fact, he kept remind me of that thought when we did not agree. It didn't help me one bit because I thought if he would only listen to me and take my counsel, no mistakes HAD to be made!

Usually a man comes into marriage thinking that he and his wife are partners. She thinks so too. Soon she has different opinions than he does about certain things. She doesn't do them the way he does. She doesn't even WANT to do things his way, and he doesn't want to do them her way either.

Now the man says, "I'm the head of this home, and therefore I make the final decisions." Where did the partnership go?

As time goes on he makes more and more decisions she

doesn't agree with. Then he starts deciding things about both their lives without even telling her about them. She feels left out, useless, not needed, and pushed away and behind her husband. Then her thinking is, "Well, if he doesn't care about me, I'll just do my own thing!" Instead of staying behind her husband, she steps out in front of him.

He can't figure out what is wrong. He says, "I've done everything for that woman, and now I can't do a thing with her. She is so self-willed [and she is]; she doesn't care about me at all." He doesn't realize that he was self-willed first.

Now, neither of them is right. You see, a woman cannot stand by her man unless he lets her. When a man puts his wife behind him she will take it only so long. Then she steps out in front of him. Neither one of them understand true submission or true headship. They do not realize that the husband and wife roles are given by God so both will have their needs met and feel fulfillment in their lives.

Chuck and I progressed through the scenario I've described just short of the place where the woman steps out and does her own thing. It was at that point that I prayed for our hearts to be opened to one another. It was then that one of the "new things" the Lord taught us was about headship and submission.

We learned that true headship is serving, and true submission is giving. Both mean the same thing. God never wants us to lord it over another person, whether our mate or anyone else.

In Luke 22:25-27 the Lord is talking to His disciples about leadership. He talks about the Gentiles who lord it over those whom they lead. He says that He doesn't want it to be that way with them. Instead, He says, let the greatest among them be as the youngest, and the leader as the servant. He asks them who is greater, the one reclining at the table or the one serving? "Is it not the one who reclines at table?" He says. "But I am among you as the one who serves."

Jesus Christ's example of true headship — true leadership — is not lording it over another, but serving. It's thinking of yourself last, not first (Mark 9:35). It is giving, not taking (Mark 10:43-45). It is thinking of yourself the way the Lord says — as a bondservant of God, doing only the will of the master. A bondservant has this attitude to his master — "What pleases you, Lord, pleases me." Jesus Christ came to earth to be the bondservant of His Father (Philippians 2:7), and that is what we should be also.

Submission also is another form of serving. Again Jesus Christ is our example. Jesus says, "I can do nothing on My own initiative...*I do not seek My own will but the will of Him who sent Me*" (John 5:30). He also says, "He who sent Me is with Me; He has not left Me alone, for *I always do the things that are pleasing to Him*" (John 8:29). The Lord is our example for both leadership and submission.

I think it is significant that Jesus Christ had authority (John 5:22), but did not use that authority unless it was in accordance with what the Father wanted. So it is with husbands and wives. In 1 Timothy 2:12 we are told that the wife is not to usurp authority from her husband. The Greek definition means "self-starting authority." Any wife has authority to act if she knows what her husband's heart is. Wives are to honor their husbands and do only those things that are pleasing to them, remembering the Lord's example. We read in Ephesians 5:21, "Be subject to one another in the fear of Christ." So husbands are to please their wives by submitting to them also. In other words, being subject to each other because we love the Lord, because we are in awe of the Lord and do not want to be disobedient to Him.

Both husband and wife are told to submit. Ephesians 5:25 tells us HOW the husband is to submit to his wife. It is by loving her just as Christ loved the church and gave Himself up for her. Both husband and wife submit to each other by giving up their lives for one another. Both live to please their mate.

What do we do when we have goals that the other partner does not have, does not want, and does not want to participate in? If we are going to serve one another, then neither one of us is going to do anything that displeases our partner. When men are in a business partnership, they confer together, decide to act or not to act. They do not make independent decisions. It is no different in a marriage. Chuck and I like to think of ourselves as two kings ruling together. When heads of countries get together for meetings, they elect one to be the chairman. That chairman is responsible for keeping order, but makes no decisions on his own. He treats all of the other heads of state with respect and deference. They are all honored equally. It is the same between Chuck and I. We both have different roles, they are both important roles, and one is not inferior to the other. Therefore, if we follow Christ's example and commands, the husband cannot lord it over his wife, nor can the wife usurp authority and lord it over her husband. Again, obedience is the key.

Chuck and I had to learn this the hard way. I've mentioned before that when we moved to our present house, Chuck became the supreme decision-maker in goals that he wanted. They were goals involving money, either giving it away or spending it; or they were goals he could not do without my help. When I did not agree with his goals, even though I told him how I felt, he went ahead and did what he wanted to anyway. It drove us apart as a team.

During this time we both wanted to be obedient, though

we didn't know what it meant to be a team. When we talked about the various goals, we discussed whether Chuck's ideas were from the Lord. He did not want to displease me, but he also wanted to "get on with his life." At that time he thought his goals were more important than our relationship. I thought our relationship was more important.

After three or four years it was so miserable for both of us that Chuck told the Lord he would not do one more thing unless I was for it. Chuck decided he would let the Lord speak through me to him. He calls this his Red Sea Experience. He considered logically what the Lord had done — how He had made our bodies so intricate and wonderful, how He had hung the moon and stars, how He opened the Red Sea to save the Israelites from the Egyptians. He decided that if God could do all that, He was big enough to change my heart to agree with his heart if we were ever to do anything again. Chuck says he thought he would be playing tennis for the rest of his life because I never wanted to do anything else he wanted to do. That took total commitment to the Lord, and also to me. Chuck made this decision on the basis of the Lord's command to husbands in Ephesians 5:29 to "love their wives as their own bodies. He who loves his own wife loves himself; for no one ever hated his own flesh, but nourishes and cherishes it, just as Christ also does the church."

Chuck learned that in Greek the word for "nourish" means to bring to full maturity, and "cherish" means to create a warm atmosphere. If a man nourishes and cherishes his wife, he will create a warm atmosphere in which his wife can be brought to full maturity. Most men create the warm atmosphere for themselves, so they can grow and be comfortable. They don't know that headship in marriage means serving their wives, rather than themselves.

In his first letter to the Thessalonian Christians the apostle Paul tells them that they are known for their labor of love. The only evidence of love is action, but that action has to be with the right attitude. I was deeply touched to think Chuck would deny himself to keep us a team. Since that encounter with the Lord, Chuck has always made me feel an equal partner in decision-making. I find myself wanting to serve him by agreeing with his ideas. However, he has created an atmosphere in which I can disagree if I feel I have to. Because I like to keep things as they are and he likes change, it's often been a struggle for both of us. However, if we make the decisions together, then one can't blame the other if it doesn't work out.

Our experience has been that when Chuck gives his opinion, I take it as an opinion. But when I give my opinion, Chuck takes it as a command. The women I've asked about this seem to have the same experience. All we want to do is talk it over, but the minute we give our opinion our husbands say with agitation, "Well, it was JUST my opinion — so have it your way!" Wait a minute — let's talk! But they are silent.

This is where we should think ahead before we blurt out our words. When I have a different opinion than Chuck, sometimes I handle it right (I wish it were more often), and this is how: I preface my remarks with a statement like, "Chuck, this is how I feel, but you must do what you think is right." This takes the defensiveness out of him and he is free to listen to me, for he doesn't think I am telling him what to do. The safety factor for me is his commitment not to go ahead with any of his ideas unless we are in agreement. Even before we had this commitment, when I remembered to preface my opinions this way he was free to hear.

It's important to know how to talk to our husbands, because of their fear of failure and their fear of being dominated by a woman. I believe that when we wives do not obey the Lord and do what He tells us to do for our husbands, their fears are realized. The wife is told in Ephesians 5, Colossians 3, Titus 2, 1 Peter 3, and 1 Timothy 2 to be in submission to her husband. Submission is *honor* we pay to our husbands, because God has given them the position of headship. The husband is responsible to God in that position. He has to honor the Lord just as we have to honor him. When we do not give the position true value by continually usurping authority, we are dominating; we are taking over. Because of this, the man's fear of being dominated by a woman is realized.

Wives are also told to "reverence" their husbands. The Amplified Bible translates this reverence like this in Ephesians 5:33 —

> And let the wife see that she respects and reverences her husband — that she notices him, regards him, honors him, prefers him, venerates and esteems him; and that she defers to him, praises him, and loves and admires him exceedingly.

When we are obedient and build him up in this manner, there is no way he is going to feel like a failure, or that he is being dominated by a woman. Knowing these are his two great fears gives us an understanding of him that helps us love and serve him the way he needs to be served. We need to take the focus off ourselves and put it on our mate. Then the final outcome will be what we wanted in the beginning — to be listened to and treated as an equal.

If this doesn't happen, the responsibility is still ours to do what the Lord says, no matter how our partner is acting.

First Peter tells us that we can win our husbands by our behavior without discussion. It is our BEHAVIOR that is going to tell our husbands that we honor and respect them, not what we say. The Lord knows that when we are angry we do not hear each other anyway. But when our behavior is respectful and honoring to our husband, he cannot blame his disobedience on us. He must look at himself. I just had a conversation with a godly man who told me his wife's behavior was the key to working out their problems. He said that as she was obedient and acted out godliness to him, he was forced to look at his own faults and deal with them.

When Chuck was making all of the family decisions, I became sadder and sadder. In fact, I'm sure I was in some sort of depression. I felt everyday that I just couldn't get through it. I was so tired.

We heard Gary Smalley speak, and he told how he had wounded his wife Norma's spirit during the early years of their marriage by being the decision-maker instead of a servant-leader. I realized that this had happened to us also. Gary explained that a wife's wounded spirit can be opened up again when he asks for her forgiveness. I knew that this was what Chuck should do for me. Of course, I told him that he should do it. He would not. He said later he just couldn't.

As he looks back, he feels the Lord was teaching him about marriage, not money and investments. At the same time, the Lord was teaching me that no matter what Chuck did, I could have peace and serenity if I would only be obedient to Him.

This impasse continued for several months. I didn't like Chuck very much or think that his jokes were funny. It was a time of quiet truce, but no real fellowship.

The day came when I just felt hopeless. Then the Lord brought to my mind Luke 6:36-37 —

Be merciful, just as your Father is merciful. And do not pass
judgment and you will not be judged; and do not condemn,
and you shall not be condemned; pardon, and you will be
pardoned.

In my heart I was judging Chuck. I was thinking of what "he"
had to do to make me happy. I wasn't being merciful. In fact, I
was bound up in my own expectations. I was condemning him
because he wasn't doing what I thought he should. I was
putting all the responsibility on him when in fact I should not
have been concerned about him at all. I was the one responsible to do things God's way.

When I realized what I was doing, I told the Lord that if
Chuck NEVER asked me to forgive him, it would be okay.
There was a peace that settled over me and I knew that God
had blessed my decision. You see, the phrase in the verse that
says "pardon and you will be pardoned" can also be translated
as "release others and you will be released," or "set at liberty
and you will be set at liberty." That is what happened to me. I
had let a root of bitterness take hold. By forgiving, I had
destroyed the root of bitterness, and the plant of anger died.

Within the week, Chuck called me from work and asked
me out for dinner. He said he wanted to open up my spirit.
The Lord knew that I needed to be healed by Him before He
would move Chuck to ask for my forgiveness.

I believe there are many, many hurts that could be healed
by the Lord alone if people would stop blaming others for their
problems and see the importance of their own responsibility to
forgive one another.

I was thrilled when Chuck realized I was an equal partner
in our marriage. It's wonderful when a husband realizes that
he and his wife are a team. Independent decisions can be

made before marriage, but never again after. Chuck and I know we are a team — we are in covenant with each other. We no longer think only of ourselves. Neither of us is an independent decision-maker; we are learning how to mesh our goals together and serve each other.

Just as a man and woman are not independent of the other (1 Corinthians 11:11), I believe Scripture teaches also that wives are in the supportive role in marriage. In 1 Corinthians 11:9 we are told that the woman was created for the man's sake, not the man for the woman. As I've thought about this I realize that I am happier in the supportive role than being out on my own. I know this is not true of every woman I have talked with, but I believe we women all know that our husbands cannot reach their potential without us. The supportive role must be important or God would not put us in this position.

We get off the track so easily because we hear so much on radio and television and read in print that we cannot be happy and be "just a homemaker." If men were bombarded with the media telling them they were missing out by working, and heard the same message year after year after year, they'd all want to stay home. I think it is because the primary role given women has been put down so much that "Women's Lib" has come about to prove to everyone that women have worth.

I do not believe Scripture teaches that a woman must work at home only, or that only women who are fulltime homemakers are supportive of their husbands. But I believe it's easier to adapt to a husband's schedule and needs if fulltime homemaking is chosen.

I made it my goal to be a homemaker when the kids were growing up, and it is one of my goals now. I've found that when I am home I can do anything I want. I am in charge of my own time. I can keep up my home, and plan any number of other things to do. When our children were small, before they were in school, I would load them into the car along with my ironing and go to a friend's house. We would iron and visit while the two sets of children played. Then we would all have lunch together and the children would take their naps. The little ones had a wonderful time and so did we. At other times we would knit, can fruit, sew, or just talk and support each other. It was a wonderful time of life. I would not trade that kind of life any day for working outside the home.

Now that our children are grown and we have grandchildren who need our time, it's just as important to be free. I like to be able to plan meals and have the family over. I wouldn't feel like doing it if I had a fulltime job. I tried working for a short time, but I feel I can accomplish my goals by staying home.

I have had my goals listed in my notebook since 1983. I read them occasionally to make sure I keep on track. Here they are:

To know God.
To obey Him.
To love my husband with action and words.
To love Tim, Bev, and Deb with action and words (and now my daughter-in-law Tammie and our two grand-daughters Kjersten and Brooke).
To be a Bible teacher who walks as she talks.
To be able to say, "Imitate me as I follow the Lord."

This last year I determined to learn to quilt, and I've made three pillows and one baby quilt for Brooke. I have a continuing goal to knit baby sweaters to have on hand as they are needed for showers — and whenever Kjersten or Brooke out-grow theirs. I am not one who can just sit without having my hands busy. I find I can listen better while I quilt or knit.

I have a continuing goal to be looking for birthday and Christmas presents as I do my normal shopping. I have a closet filled with gifts waiting to be given. This takes pressure off if there is a time crunch at the same time I would have to be shopping.

My goals revolve around my relationships with others or with the Lord. My goals revolve around *being* — being a wife, mother, grandmother, and friend. Chuck's goals usually involve *doing* — building furniture in his workshop, construct-ing horseshoe pits, building an exercise house, making a video, writing a book, putting in a sport court, putting a cover over the tennis court (we've never agreed on this one yet).

As we've grown older I've seen Chuck's goals change more toward relationships too. Time for me, time for our chil-dren, time for grandchildren, time for counseling, time for friends, time to be with the Lord.

Because the Bible tells older women to teach the younger women I have made it my goal to study and teach Bible study groups instead of working for pay. I have chosen to be in con-tact with my students — who soon become friends — instead of working for pay. I have chosen to have quiet times to refuel my soul instead of working for pay. I have been able to choose because Chuck has enabled me, and I know there are many who have no choice because of economics. But if the choice is yours, I'd recommend being a homemaker.

Chuck and I do not set our minds on goals the other is not for. Chuck is the dreamer, the idea person, so I believe he has the harder time because he thinks up so MANY goals. But he doesn't set his mind to accomplish these goals unless we both agree. I do not do anything he is against, and he honors me the same way.

We put each other first. We are FOR the other. We try to help each other fulfill our goals. We are a team.

THOUGHTS TO CONSIDER

Have you decided to walk beside your husband — and not in front, concerned with your goals only?

Have you talked about this with him?

Before reading this chapter, were you aware that headship and submission involve serving your mate and not yourself?

Are you aware that both husband and wife are told to submit to each other?

Would you be able to recall the Scripture (and tell it to others) about how Christ is the example of true headship and true submission?

Can you explain the characteristics of a bondservant?

Remember: Submission does not strip you of authority nor equality.

Do you do anything — spend money, or make decisions — when you know your mate is against it?

Do you think of your marriage partner as a teammate, or are you just two people living in the same house and having the same children?

When you act out your love to your mate, do you have a good attitude?

Your reverence for your husband means honoring him and building him up.

Remember: Your obedience will keep your husband from experiencing two fears in his life — fear of failure, and fear of being dominated by a woman.

Are you obedient despite your husband's disobedience?

Are you held in bondage because of your expectations?

Have you forgiven and released those who have hurt you, either recently or in the past?

SCRIPTURES TO KNOW

LUKE 22:25-27
And He said to them, "The kings of the Gentiles lord it over them; and those who have authority over them are called 'Benefactors.' But not so with you, but let him who is the greatest among you become as the youngest, and the leader as the servant. For who is greater, the one who reclines at table, or the one who serves? Is it not the one who reclines at table? But I am among you as the one who serves."

from EPHESIANS 5:21-33, Amplified Bible
Be subject to one another out of reverence for Christ, the Messiah, the Anointed One. Wives, be subject — be submissive and adapt yourselves — to your own husbands as [a service] to the Lord....

Husbands love your wives, as Christ loved the church and gave Himself up for her....

Even so husbands should love their wives as [being in a sense] their own bodies. He who loves his own wife loves himself. For no man ever hated his own flesh, but nourishes and carefully protects and cherishes it, as Christ does the church....

However, let each man of you (without exception) love his wife as [being in a sense] his very own self; and let the wife see that she respects and reverences her husband — that she notices him, regards him, honors him, prefers him, venerates and esteems him; and that she defers to him, praises him, and loves and admires him exceedingly.

LUKE 6:36-38

Be merciful, just as your Father is merciful. And do not pass judgment and you will not be judged; and do not condemn, and you shall not be condemned; pardon, and you will be pardoned.

Give and it will be given to you; good measure, pressed down, shaken together, running over, they will pour into your lap. For whatever measure you deal out to others, it will be dealt to you in return.

Whatever you do, do your work heartily, for the Lord
rather than for men; knowing that from the Lord you will receive
the reward of the inheritance. It is the Lord Christ whom you serve.
COLOSSIANS 3:23-24

TODAY WAS THE DAY — nothing was going to keep Chuck
from working on the film he was doing for a mission in Puerto
Rico. We had flown there several months before and filmed.
This was going to be a tool to let everyone back home know
what the missionaries were doing. Chuck had been so busy
with his everyday work that he hadn't had time to work on it.
So he and our daughter Bev decided today was the day, and
she was going to help him.

About mid-morning I received a call from some dear
friends. Their daughter was related by marriage to the agents
for Roy Rogers and Dale Evans. Dale and Roy were in town,
my friend told me, and she asked if we were free for lunch. I
had read everything Dale Evans Rogers had written, and I
would have loved to go to lunch with them — but Chuck had
told me that "nothing" was going to keep him from working on

that film. So I told them how sorry we were, but we just couldn't.

Looking back, it seems crazy that I would not have called Chuck and given him the option of going to lunch with them. However, though neither of us realized it at the time, Chuck was using his work to protect himself from doing anything he did not want to do. He'd said he HAD to get the film done. I believed him, so made the decision not to go to lunch on my own, thinking it was a decision he would make.

But when I told him about it later he said, "I think I would like to have gone." Since then we've regretted not being able to get to know the Rogers. Their lives reflect Jesus Christ, and it would have been very, very special to share the Lord with them.

But Chuck didn't have his work done, and he felt unsettled until he did. We believe God has given men the primary responsibility to provide and work for the family. In Genesis 3:17-19, God said to the first man,

> Cursed is the ground because of you; in toil you shall eat of it all the days of your life. Both thorns and thistles it shall grow for you; and you shall eat the plants of the field; by the sweat of your face you shall eat bread....

Because God gave the job of providing food to Adam, not Eve, we believe that this is a man's primary concern in life. Therefore, a man's work is the main area in which he expresses his personality. He needs work to feel worthwhile.

Because a man's work is so important in his life, many women feel ignored and taken for granted. It seems their husband is more interested in his work than in them. I think this is why God has given so many relational instructions to men.

They do not naturally think of relationships like women do. Their focus is their work. And this is right, as long as it stays in balance.

To help them stay in balance, here are some of the relational instructions the Lord has given men, in Ephesians 5, Colossians 3, and 1 Peter 3:

Love your wife. ("Love" is action with the right attitude.)

Nourish and cherish your wife. (The Greek word here means to create a warm atmosphere in which your wife can be brought to full maturity.)

Do not embitter your wife.

Live with your wife in an understanding way.

Grant her honor as a fellow-heir of the grace of life ("honor" means to value, to pay a price for).

My work is to be the guardian of my home, according to Paul's instructions in Titus 2:4-5.

Older women...encourage the young women to love their husbands, to love their children, to be sensible, pure, workers at home, kind, being subject to their own husbands, that the word of God may not be dishonored.

The term "workers at home" can be translated "guardians of the home." *The Amplified Bible* translates this as "homemakers." We believe the home reflects the woman's personality because God has given primary care of the home to her. God tells women, not men, to take care of the home. He tells men, not women, to provide for the family.

My experience is that I feel unsettled until there are clean clothes in the drawers, the ironing is done, and there is food in the house. My responsibility, my work, is the upkeep of the home, just as Chuck's responsibility is to work to earn money, so we can have the clothes, food, and shelter we need.

No matter what else I do, if my home is not in order, I feel confusion. That is one of the reasons I have a hard time getting to writing. It seems that it is late morning each day before I sit down at this computer to write. First it's the breakfast dishes, then the bed to make, then of course I have to repair myself each day, and any number of things that need doing — flowers to water, rooms to straighten, laundry, and so on.

I have a desire to keep my home clean and beautifully decorated. I don't want it to be a showplace, but a place of warmth and comfort, where all who come will feel at home and cared for. I want it to be a haven of rest for Chuck, our children, and our guests.

In this day and age of Women's Lib I feel that a misunderstanding has taken place. Most young men now feel that the wife should work and help earn money also. I don't see this idea backed up in Scripture, nor do I think it is how the Lord had it planned. I've talked to many gals who want so desperately to stay home with their children but their husbands do not believe they are doing their fair share if they do. They do not know they are the ones who are commanded to be earning a living and their wives are only commanded to care for their home and their family.

Having both parents working, in my opinion, has caused a lot of problems that would not occur if Mom stayed home. Just think — there'd be better meals, a cleaner house, less stress, and a wife who has energy to be flirty and fun. We've listened to the world, and we think that both husband and wife have to work in order to have "things" while their relationship goes down the drain.

The relationship suffers not only because the man feels his wife should work, but also because so often he feels the housework is only woman's work too. In her book *Women and Fatigue,* Dr. Holly Atkinson quotes a woman who says, "The only thing the women's movement has earned women is the right to be perpetually tired." Dr. Atkinson adds, "When a man comes home tired from work and finds dishes piled up in the sink and children's toys all over the living-room floor, he might or might not clean up. But if he chooses to ignore the mess and put up his feet, *he's unlikely to feel guilty or to feel he's denying a part of his own identity.* Many women, on the other hand, end up scrubbing the kitchen floor at 11 P.M. after everyone else has gone to bed — even if they have a business breakfast at 7:30 A.M. *Men don't internalize housework; it's not involved with their self-concept.* Even fairly progressive women will praise their husbands for 'helping' with the housework, implying it's actually the woman's primary responsibility" (italics mine).

We know from Scripture that housework IS the woman's primary responsibility. This does not mean a woman cannot work outside the home. She can — because we see working women throughout Scripture. But we as women need to weigh the negatives as well as the positives before we give up our freedom and decide to work both in the marketplace and at home, for instead of just one job, we double our workload.

When Chuck and I bought the advertising agency, I worked at the office for a short time. Of course I had the liberty to go home if the kids were sick and I could attend my weekly Bible study. But because there was so much to do, and I was responsible for a certain part of it, there was pressure on me from both the home and the office.

One day at about 5 P.M. Chuck was giving me instructions. I started to cry because I was tired, and it was the end of the day and he was giving me more to do. He said, "Secretaries don't cry!"

"I know," I exclaimed, "but wives do!"

We both stopped and laughed, but the pressure continued — not necessarily from Chuck but certainly from the circumstances.

After several months we hired someone to take my place. It was wonderful to be home again. Chuck came in one evening and said, "I feel so secure when you are home!" I'm sure he felt more cared for because things were under control again. Dinner was ready when he arrived home, and best of all the kids were not left to themselves after school. I know children learn responsibility from the chores they have to do if mothers have to work, but I think God's best is to have Mom at home and present while chores are learned under her supervision. As for me, I would choose to be home any day.

In a recent issue of the *Ladies Home Journal*, Barbara Walters is quoted as saying, "I believe it is possible to have a great marriage and a great career, or to have a great marriage and great children, or to have great children and a great career; but it's awfully tough to have all three at the same time."

In the same issue, actress Candice Bergen, who has a three-year-old daughter, admits she often can't cope with it all. "I'm so tired," she confessed. "And I'm crabby. There are enough nights when my husband and I are reduced to eating cheese rinds and tuna fish out of the can because we don't have anything in the refrigerator. I can't get the energy to cook, and I think, *I'm going to lose this man over a tuna sandwich!*"

Also in that issue is an article titled "No Sex Please" by Dorothy Glass Weiss. She quotes a married woman named Jeannie, age thirty-one, an urban planner in New York City: "I drag myself home some nights so wrung out I can barely get myself into bed. If my husband approaches me even for a chaste kiss, I find myself thinking, Please don't come any-where within ten feet of me. I don't want to — can't possibly — deal with one more demand.

It takes a lot of energy to run a home and raise children, just as it takes a lot of energy for the man to work. I learned when I worked in the business world how important it is to come home to a quiet haven, with everything in order and under control. The children for the most part did very well when I was working, but there were days when chaos was reigning when Chuck and I arrived home. I was just too tired to handle it well, and so was Chuck. In our marriage — in our situation — one of us needed to be home to welcome the other with a hot meal and tender loving care. And that some-one had to be me, not only because I believed God wanted me there, but also because I wanted to be there.

I found more quotes from the *Ladies Home Journal* in an article titled "Stay-at-Home Moms Speak Out." Shelli Rehmert of Marquette, Nebraska, states, "My husband and I have agreed to live within a very limited budget in order that I may be the sole caregiver of our children. Although I do not receive a salary, I consider my "career" one of the most satisfying, ful-filling, and at times stressful jobs in society. Homemaking is an exciting and rewarding job and should be viewed as more than a leave of absence from society."

Cathy Cornell of Columbus, Ohio, says, "I am a mother of two children under age four, and am a full-time college student. Our income is about $20,000 per year, since I do not hold a job outside the home. I am away from my children about 15 hours per week. We drive cars that are several years old and rusty. We own an older house that we are remodeling bit by bit. But we are happy with our choice, and we are doing quite well with God's help. I want the American people to know that it is possible to have children who are cared for by a stay-at-home parent."

Paula Grier of Tulsa, Oklahoma, writes, "I found the 'Ask the Kids' section of your day-care article heartbreaking. Seven of the eight children quoted wish that Mom or Dad would spend more time with them. We have a generation of parents intent on fulfilling their self-centered wants at the cost of their children's very real needs."

I believe work is more than being employed outside the home. There are different kinds of work. A woman's work DOES and always will include relationships in the family. It is very important to "be" a wife, mother, grandmother, friend. Working in business is not all there is to life. I believe it is the women who stay home who may have the most influence in the world. After all, most of life has to do with relationships. If there is no time, relationships falter and fail. It takes time to "be" everything you need to be to your husband, children, and grandchildren. It takes time to be a friend. It takes time to study the Bible so good, sound counsel can be given to those in need. It takes time to read and be a resource to tell others about books that can help them. It just takes time.

I would challenge all women to ask the Lord what He wants you to do. Maybe He DOES want you in the business world. But maybe He wants you to be a fulltime guardian of the home...and a friend to your children. As we've seen, the book of Titus tells mothers to love their husbands and children.

This love is a friendship love, the kind of love that makes the other feel liked and admired, the love that plays and has fun. It is difficult to find enough time or energy to work outside the home if you are going to love in this way.

I've often wondered if some husbands put pressure on their wives to work because they think they are wasting so much time. The house is not clean, the wash is not done, dinner is late. The husband wonders what she's been doing. Has she been on the phone with friends all day instead of getting her home in order? Maybe she is just not organized. Whatever, it would be hard for ME to be a husband and have my wife at home not getting her work done.

This brings me to Colossians 3:23-24.

> Whatever you do, do your work heartily, as for the Lord rather than for men; knowing that from the Lord you will receive the reward of the inheritance. It is the Lord Christ whom you serve.

It's not easy to be at home all day with little ones. It's not easy to keep up a home day after day. It's not easy to wash dishes that you know will be dirty all too soon again. And so we must ask, "What is the motivation for our lives?" Is it serving ourselves or the Lord? If it is serving the Lord, and He tells wives and mothers to be guardians of our homes, then let's do it. Let's don't be thinking, "It sure would be easier if we worked instead of raised the kids." And if you ARE working outside your home, what is your attitude? Are you working for the Lord? Wherever you are, whatever you are doing, make sure your motivation is to serve the Lord and not yourself.

Oswald Chambers says this about sacrifice:

Sacrifice means giving up something that we mind giving up. We talk of giving up our possessions; none of them are ours to give up. "A man's life consisteth not in the abundance of the things which he possesseth." Our Lord tells us to give up the one thing that is going to hurt badly — that is, our right to ourselves.

Now that our children are raised, I must tell you that it is worth every moment I spent with them. It is worth every moment I spent with Chuck too, for now it is just the two of us. If he and I had not invested in each other, what would we have today?

I'm so glad we chose to serve God, and because of that, each other.

THOUGHTS TO CONSIDER

A wife and mother's primary work is being the guardian of the home.

A husband's and father's primary work is making a living (i.e., earning money) to provide the shelter, clothing, and food for his family.

Are "things" too important to you? Would you be willing to be a homemaker, giving up money to buy "things" in exchange for more time to care for your home and family?

Do you and your husband agree that you are doing what the Lord wants you to do, whether it is working outside the home or being a homemaker?

Are you feeling pressured beyond measure by working in the business world and caring for your home and family at the same time. Have you considered being a fulltime homemaker?

Would your husband like to have you stay at home rather that working outside it?

Do you feel sorry for yourself (whether you work fulltime at home, or in the business world)? Or do you work heartily for the Lord?

Is your heart motivation to honor the Lord no matter what you do?

Are you willing to do whatever the Lord tells you?

Ask the Lord to take away from your thinking any repeated thoughts that are not from Him.

Are you discerning the Lord's will in your life by making sure you are not disobeying any principles He has given in Scripture? Ask for His peace in your heart before deciding to do something. (Ephesians 2:14 tells us, "He Himself is our peace.")

SCRIPTURES TO KNOW

EPHESIANS 6:7-8

With good will render service, as to the Lord, and not to men, knowing that whatever good thing each one does, this he will receive back from the Lord, whether slave or free.

COLOSSIANS 3:23-25

Whatever you do, do your work heartily, as for the Lord rather than for men; knowing that from the Lord you will receive the reward of the inheritance. It is the Lord Christ whom you serve. For he who does wrong will receive the consequences of the wrong which he has done, and that without partiality.

LAMENTATIONS 3:22-23

The Lord's lovingkindnesses indeed never cease,
For His compassions never fail.
They are new every morning;
Great is Thy faithfulness.

2 CHRONICLES 16:9

For the eyes of the Lord move to and fro throughout the earth that He may strongly support those whose heart is completely His.

HIS GIFTS & MINE

As each one has received a special gift, employ it in serving
one another, as good stewards of the manifold grace of God. Whoever speaks, let him speak, as it were, the utterances of God;
whoever serves, let him do so as by the strength which God supplies;
so that in all things God may be glorified through Jesus Christ,
to whom belongs the glory and dominion forever and ever. Amen.
1 PETER 4:10-11

CHUCK AND I had just finished the week at Bill Gothard's
seminar — the week that changed Chuck's life forever, and
because of that, mine also. Chuck had surrendered all of himself and his life to the Lord even though he feels he became a
Christian when he was nine years old. He says he gave all of
himself — one hundred percent — but he told the Lord that he
knew he would never teach because he had a soft voice, and
got teary easily. It came to Chuck's mind, however, that the
Lord said He did His best work through a person's weakness.
So — "everything" was to be the Lord's.

Immediately Chuck was asked to teach a short lesson to
some college-age people. He had been so struck with Psalm 1

---

that he chose that as his topic. He was great! — or, I should say, the Lord was great through him.

As time went on, Chuck saturated himself with the Word of God. Then, when he was asked to speak, he would tell them what he had been learning and how he had been obedient in various circumstances, and what had been the result of that obedience. He always told them when and how he had failed, but he also told them the victory he had when he did things the Lord's way. People just loved to hear him teach. He was practical. They knew he understood where they were living. He was open. He was real.

Chuck and I taught children's church for eighteen years. We loved the fourth-, fifth-, and sixth-grade kids. But then it was time to move on. We were asked to teach a young married group. *How could that be?* we wondered. *We were young marrieds ourselves just yesterday!* But it was true — we were old enough to teach it. I say "we," but Chuck is the one who stood up front, though we had a plan that included me. Whenever I had a Scripture to back up what Chuck was saying, I was to raise my hand and he would call on me. Chuck based everything he said on Scripture, but somehow I could always find more to add to it. With Chuck teaching there was always a lot of discussion and many laughs.

There were also changed lives. People started sharing stories with us about their obedience. Chuck taught one day about asking forgiveness when you have offended someone. He also challenged them to do something nice for their "enemies." One gal came back to class telling us that she had never gotten along with the neighbors in her cul-de-sac. There was terrible tension between them. So she baked each neighbor a pie, carried it to them individually, and asked for their forgiveness. She came to class beaming. Everyone else

HIS GIFTS & MINE

beamed too, and rejoiced at her renewed relationships and the peace she felt. The neighbors loved the pies, and were friends again — all because Chuck talked to the class so convincingly from the Scriptures. It was encouraging and fun to see changed lives.

When we were teaching children's church, Chuck would study his lesson on Saturday night and his teaching was wonderful the next day. I would study for the whole week and often felt I needed more time. We just did not approach this teaching thing the same way.

For years, because I did not feel I knew the Bible well enough, I had a Bible study for women in our home using tapes by Kay Arthur. When the tape was over, I would share an experience from my life that would go along with what Kay had taught. Also, I would get the women involved by asking questions that pertained to the lesson. It was a wonderful time of sharing and getting to know each other and the Lord better. Then Kay began writing Precept Upon Precept Bible Studies, which involved five hours of homework each week. She showed me her work and said that from now on she always planned to teach this way. That meant that I would have to put more effort into my Bible study. It had been so easy up to this point — just listen to her tapes, read the Scriptures, ask some questions, and that was it. But now there would have to be real commitment!

I told my class I thought we should do this study. They thought it was a good idea too, but the class size went from about twenty down to four students, one listener, and myself. I did not want to study this way, and yet I *did* want to because I knew the Lord wanted me to.

That, I believe, was the turning point in my spiritual life, because it opened up my life to the power of the Word. In

139

The Amplified Bible, Hebrews 4:12 reads,

> For the Word that God speaks is alive and full of power —
> making it active, operative, energizing and effective; it is
> sharper than any two-edged sword, penetrating to the divid-
> ing line of the breath of life (soul) and [the immortal] spirit,
> and of the joints and marrow [that is, of the deepest parts of
> our nature], exposing and sifting and analyzing and judging
> the very thoughts and purposes of the heart.

Unless we are in the Word ourselves, we will not be trans-
formed. Our minds will not be renovated or renewed, as
Romans 12:2 tells us they can be.

It was not easy, but it was wonderful. Each of us learned so
much. We learned how to observe a passage, how to mark
repeated words and then ask the who, what, where, when,
why, and how questions about them. Amazing! A simple thing
like a colored pencil marking the repeated words could tell me
what the subject of the passage was. How I had struggled
before that!

We learned how to compare Scripture with Scripture to
make sure our interpretation was correct, because one Scripture cannot contradict another. We learned how to find the
Greek or Hebrew definition for words, and to follow these
exact words through the Scriptures. This process showed us
how to cross-reference verses and subjects, and follow a train
of thought through the Bible. We found the Holy Spirit giving
us the same insights as great Bible scholars. We started with
Scripture, and stayed with Scripture until we had exhausted
each step of study (observation, interpretation, application)
BEFORE we went to commentaries, and therefore the Lord was
able to speak to us individually, instead of our trying to fit

Scripture into preconceived beliefs. And because I learned to study this way, I can write my own Bible studies and not have to depend on another person's study in order to teach. I believe this is how the Word stays new and fresh in my life.

As an aside, I also believe that to KNOW the Word is not enough. One must also apply the principles and obey the commands given. When a person knows the Word without incorporating it into their lives, a hard heart can result: a heart that says, "Oh, I know that...why do I have to hear it again?" This person doesn't realize that the reason he must hear it again is because it has not become a part of him yet.

From all of the above, you may have guessed that my gift is teaching. And from Chuck's ability to get people to "walk their talk," you have probably guessed that Chuck has the gift of exhortation.

No matter what our gift, it is the Lord who gives the gift, the ministry, and the effect or result. 1 Corinthians 12:4-7 tells us,

> Now there are varieties of gifts, but the same Spirit. And there are varieties of ministries, and the same Lord. And there are varieties of effects, but the same God who works all things in all persons. But to each one is given the manifestation of the Spirit for the common good.

So we see...
                    many gifts...the same Spirit
                 many ministries...the same Lord
                  many effects...the same God

The Father, Son, and Holy Spirit are all involved in giving us our gifts, and in what we do with them. And we know from verse seven that they are given for the common good, to help each other.

I have found that when we have a disagreement on how to present Scripture for a lesson we are teaching, it is usually because of the way we see things through our gifts. Chuck says he just tells them what he reads. I say that you don't always know what you've read if you don't know the exact meaning of the Greek or Hebrew words and the tense of the verbs. Chuck says just "do" it. I say you can't just hang *doing* on thin air; you have to build a foundation for it. You first have to *be*, and by *be* I mean knowing who you are in Christ, and the power you have in Christ, and the strength He gives us because "we have been freed from sin" (Romans 6:7). We HAVE the power to be obedient. God has saved us not only from paying the penalty for sin, but also from the power of sin in our life. We CAN be obedient, therefore we MUST be obedient.

In 1 John 2:3 we are told,

And by this we know that we have come to know Him, if we keep His commandments.

My motivation in teaching is to make sure people know why they can be obedient. I don't want them thinking they have an excuse to sin. I want them to know "how incredibly great His power is to help those who believe Him. It is that same mighty power that raised Christ from the dead..." (Ephesians 1:19-20, *The Living Bible*).

Chuck likes to teach from a list of Scriptures that pertain to the same subject. If I teach something topical, I like to have the Scriptures written out, with questions written above them in order to build my theme which leads to a specific goal. And the Scriptures I would choose to discuss are not the same as Chuck would choose. So sometimes he chooses them, and sometimes I do. Chuck likes to wing it, and I like to know exactly where I'm going. (Of course, teaching with him, one never knows exactly where one is going.) Chuck causes us to have more fun than if I taught alone.

Even after studying, I often feel I don't have anything to say. I don't feel any inspiration. When we were teaching a class on Sunday morning we would be driving to church and I would tell Chuck that I just didn't have anything to say that morning. I just felt dry! Then Chuck would open the class, say something that would spark me, and the thoughts and words would begin flowing for me. He teases me often and tells me to be sure and take a breath so he can get a word in edgewise.

Chuck uses *The Living Bible,* while I use the *New American Standard Bible.* He swears he can't understand my Bible, and I call his Bible a commentary because it is a paraphrase instead of word-for-word translation (though I find it enjoyable to read and a wonderful tool that often says it just right). Chuck does use a variety of translations when he studies.

Because Chuck loves *The Living Bible* and its plain-spoken language, when we teach side by side and have Scripture to read, he reads the passage from his Bible, then I read it from mine, and we talk about it.

Chuck used to tell me that I wasn't practical at all, meaning I never got to what the result would be in our daily life from knowing the principles we were teaching. I never could figure out why he thought that. I'd tell him that unless I said "strawberries," or something like that, he thought I wasn't practical. Then I discovered that when we teach together, I start the process of laying a foundation. I plan to lay the foundation, and then come back and build on it for our everyday walk. But before I can get to the next verse, he says, "Wait a minute — let's see how this affects our lives today." Then he goes into the DOING part of the teaching, and I haven't finished the BEING part yet. I finally realized that when we teach together he never hears me get to the doing part because he gets there first. However, when I teach alone, I do eventually get to the doing part.

It can be frustrating at times for both of us, but together I think that we are better teachers than either of us is alone. We complete each other even in this part of our lives.

When we teach together and one of us finishes a thought, we just look at each other, and that is the signal that we are through for the moment. Then too, we have been known to discuss (argue?) fine points with each other as we teach. I guess it's all rather complicated — but it works. We get lots of discussion going and there is much involvement with the audience, especially if we are teaching on a week-to-week basis.

Another gift I'm sure Chuck has is the gift of giving. Because of this gift we have had some major adjustments. People with the gift of giving often think they can fix any problem with a gift of money. On the other hand, if their mate sees a bigger picture, it can cause disagreements. I have often felt so selfish in comparison to Chuck, and yet felt the Lord did not need our money to solve this or that problem. Sometimes I agree with Chuck, but when we don't agree we have to fall back on our commitment to not make a decision unless we both agree.

It has become easier for me to give after doing a study on giving in the Bible. I have come to see that we first give ourselves completely to the Lord, and then give of our resources to Him and to others (1 Corinthians 8:5). Scripture tells us we cannot serve two masters — God and money. "For either we will hate the one and love the other, or we will hold to one and despise the other" (Matthew 6:24). Scripture also tells us that when we give to others, they will know that our "deeds are as good as our doctrine."

I like the way *The Living Bible* states it in 2 Corinthians 9:9-15 —

It is as the Scriptures say: "The godly man gives generously to the poor. His good deeds will be an honor to him forever."

For God, who gives seed to the farmer to plant, and later on, good crops to harvest and eat, will give you more and more seed to plant and will make it grow so that you can give away more and more fruit from your harvest.

Yes, God will give you much so that you can give away much, and when we take your gifts to those who need them they will break out into thanksgiving and praise to God for your help. So, two good things happen as a result of your gifts — those in need are helped, and they overflow with thanks to God. Those you help will be glad not only because of your generous gifts to themselves and to others, but they will praise God for this proof that your deeds are as good as your doctrine. And they will pray for you with deep fervor and feeling because of the wonderful grace of God shown through you.

Thank God for his Son — His Gift too wonderful for words.

I agree with Chuck that it's important to "do," but I believe we will not "do" as much as we could if we have not first learned to "be."

Chuck loves to study, counsel, and teach. I love to study and teach. I like to spend hours studying. He likes to be reading and underlining his Bible and then reading books on various subjects to help in his counseling. He does his studying and reading in short spurts of time. At one time he felt threatened by the way I studied. When he told me, I was surprised because I've never known a man who is in the Word as much as he is. He is always growing, obeying, and sharing. It's so obvious that he is doing and being all that the Lord has planned for him. We are just different.

When Chuck realized that our gifts were different, he did everything he could to help me study by buying me the right resource books. For Christmas he gave me a computer program with many resource books and different Bible translations, plus another program with the *New American Standard Bible.* He has been my greatest support.

We have talked with many couples where the wife has a speaking gift and the man has a serving gift. Because of this, the man feels inferior to his wife. He may even believe that he should be speaking and not his wife.

But 1 Peter 4:10-11 says,

As each one has received a special gift, employ it in serving one another, as good stewards of the manifold grace of God. Whoever speaks, let him speak, as it were, the utterances of God; whoever serves, let him do so as by the strength which God supplies; so that in all things God may be glorified through Jesus Christ, to whom belongs the glory and dominion forever and ever. Amen.

God has said that He is not partial (Romans 2:11). When He gave gifts to us, He gave them to build up the believers in His church. Every gift is necessary to make us work together in a successful way. Speaking and serving gifts have equal value ...equal honor.

It's a shame when a man feels inferior to his wife just because the Lord has not given them the same gift. One is not better than the other. With the differences, let's decide to serve our mates and help them fulfill the purpose for which they were created.

Let's celebrate the differences!

THOUGHTS TO CONSIDER

Gifts are given to speak God's Word and to serve God's people.

We are to use our gifts to glorify God.

When we glorify God we give a correct estimate of who He is. In other words, we obey Him because He is God, and we are in awe of Him.

No matter what our gifts, we must saturate ourselves with the Word of God.

The Word of God will transform you by renovating or renewing your mind.

God uses our gifts to build up other Christians.

God gives the gifts by His Spirit, the ministries by His Son, and the results are up to Him. Our part is to make sure our heart motivation is to glorify God.

The same gift may be used in various ways according to the purpose God has for the gift. A speaking gift may be given to teach small children, adults, or teenagers. It may be used in big groups, small groups, or one-on-one.

A serving gift may be used in big groups, small groups, or one-on-one.

The gifts of helps and service have different Greek words. Some scholars believe one describes serving in the sense of serving meals or setting up chairs or the like. The other describes ministering to another person, perhaps to someone who has a speaking gift but needs assistance and support in his or her area of ministry. This type of gift enables a person to be in the background.

1 Corinthians 14:3 tells us that "one who prophesies speaks to men for edification and exhortation and consolation." Remember that prophecy is not foretelling, but forth-telling — speaking the Word of God for building up, for encouragement and counsel, and for comfort.

Chapters in the Bible which have spiritual gifts as a main subject include Ephesians 4, 1 Peter 4, 1 Corinthians 12-14, and Romans 12.

Here is a list of books to help you understand spiritual gifts:

SPIRITUAL GIFTS — a Precept Upon Precept Bible Study
(Precept Ministries, P.O. Box 23000,
Chattanooga, Tennessee 37422)

NINETEEN GIFTS OF THE HOLY SPIRIT — by Leslie Flynn
(Victor Books)

THE HOLY SPIRIT AND HIS GIFTS — by J. Oswald Sanders (Zondervan Publishing House)

BODY LIFE — by Ray Stedman
(Regal Books Division, Gospel Light Publications)

Scriptures to Know

1 Peter 3:8-9
To sum up, let all be harmonious, sympathetic, brotherly, kind-hearted, and humble in spirit; not returning evil for evil, or insult for insult, but giving a blessing instead; for you were called for the very purpose that you might inherit a blessing.

James 1:2-5
Count it all joy, my brethren, when you encounter various trials; knowing that the testing of your faith produces endurance. And let endurance have its perfect result, that you may be perfect and complete, lacking in nothing. But if any of you lacks wisdom, let him ask of God, who gives to all men generously and without reproach, and it will be given to him.

James 1:12
Blessed is a man who perseveres under trial; for once he has been approved, he will receive the crown of life, which the Lord has promised to those who love Him.

Matthew 6:19-21
Do not [as a habit of life] lay up for yourselves treasures upon earth, where moth and rust destroy, and where thieves break in and steal; but lay up for yourselves treasures in heaven, where neither moth nor rust destroys, and where thieves do not break in or steal; for where your treasure is, there will your heart be also.

HIS *OPINIONS* & MINE

Do nothing from selfishness or empty conceit, but with humility
of mind let each of you regard one another as more important
than himself; do not merely look out for your own personal interests,
but also for the interests of others
PHILIPPIANS 2:3-4

WHEN I THINK the coffee is good, Chuck thinks it's the
worst he's ever tasted. And when I'm sure he will like a certain
dish, most often I am wrong.

If I think we should do this, he thinks we should do that. If I
think we should go late, he thinks we should go early. When
we get a room in a hotel, sometimes I don't like it and want to
ask for a different one. He thinks we should stay put.

When we first started traveling a lot, he didn't do things in
the order I thought they should be done. He always wanted to
leave for the airport much earlier than I thought necessary.
Then I would want to stop for the coffee I didn't have because
we left so early, while he wanted to get in line to get our seats.
When we arrived at our destination he wanted to get the car
first while I wanted to pick up the luggage.

And on and on.

Chuck likes to drive over the mountains to my folks' home one way. I want to go another, more beautiful way. He likes to take shortcuts and miss every stoplight he can. I like the stoplights because they make my life orderly. Of course, I like them to be green, but I don't get uptight like Chuck does when they are red.

Chuck does not want to put anyone out, so he won't send back his steak in a restaurant if it isn't done right. If mine isn't right, I'll send it back immediately — we're paying for it, and I ordered it medium-well, not rare.

When we go out to dinner, Chuck likes to sit in a booth. I much prefer a table with chairs, and by the window if possible. I like to sit and visit for a long time after dinner, but he likes to get up and go so he can "get on with his life" and "do" something.

As Chuck says, about the only thing we have in common is that we were married on the same day.

Every time we disagree, we are in a trial. The question is, How are we going to handle it? With exasperation, anger, frustration, smart remarks, sarcasm? Or are we going to be obedient and do things the Lord's way? And if we're going to respond the Lord's way, what is that way?

Scripture tells us we are to persevere and endure. In the Greek that means we are to remain in a trial in a God-honoring way. We are not to withdraw or walk away mad, nor are we to beat the thing to death by talking too much. We must not be selfish or conceited, thinking our way is the only way. We are to look out for each other's interests more than our own.

It's not just blindly doing things Chuck's way or vice versa. It is talking it out. It is finding out that Chuck assumes he will

run into construction or have a flat tire on the way to the airport, so we'd better leave home an hour and a half before our
flight takes off. It's making compromises. It's even laughing at
ourselves because we are so different.

Several verses in James 1 teach us how to go through trials
and temptations. I'd like to write them out for you and discuss
them.

> Consider it all joy, my brethren, when you encounter various
> trials; knowing that the testing of your faith produces
> endurance. And let endurance have its perfect result, that
> you may be perfect and complete, lacking in nothing.
>
> But if any of you lacks wisdom, let him ask of God who
> gives to all men generously and without reproach, and it will
> be given to him. But let him ask in faith without any doubt-
> ing, for the one who doubts is like the surf of the sea driven
> and tossed by the wind. For let not that man expect that he
> will receive anything from the Lord, being a double-minded
> man, unstable in all his ways....
>
> Blessed is the man who perseveres under trial; for once
> he has been approved, he will receive the crown of life,
> which the Lord has promised to those who love Him. Let no
> one say when he is tempted, "I am being tempted by God";
> for God cannot be tempted by evil, and He Himself does not
> tempt any one. But each is tempted when he is carried away
> and enticed by his own lust. Then when lust has conceived,
> it gives birth to sin; and when sin is accomplished, it brings
> forth death. Do not be deceived, my beloved brethren.

It is so easy to be deceived if we don't know the difference
between trials and temptations. Trials come from without.
They just happen to us. For instance, Chuck likes to set our

clocks fast, but I like them to be the exact time. When we have to get up early he likes to set the alarm to go off forty-five minutes before he actually has to get up. Then he resets the alarm three times for fifteen-minute intervals. He goes back to sleep between alarms and is thrilled to think he doesn't have to get up right away. On the other hand, I lie there wide awake, waiting for the next alarm. (When I was younger I was able to go back to sleep too. Not any more!)

Our compromise? Chuck sets the alarm, gets up after the first one, and goes into another bedroom taking the alarm clock with him. He falls back to sleep easily and goes through his usual routine while I wait for my alarm clock to sound at the actual time I need to get up.

Neither of us is right or wrong. Once again we are just different. But we both could have insisted that our way is the right way, and made the other miserable by not being considerate.

I turned this trial into a temptation once when I got up and realized it was forty minutes earlier than Chuck said it was. I was angry, made some sarcastic remark, and our day didn't start very well. However, we talked later and arrived at the solution I just told you about. Now Chuck keeps his clock faster than "really" time, and sets his alarm as often as he wants to, and I set my clock on "really" time with one alarm sounding.

The Bible tells us that trials are a test to bring about good, and to demonstrate the good quality of the one being tested. Trials produce endurance, which, again, means going through a trial in a God-honoring way. It's a keeping on keeping on. When we stay with a trial without trying to get out from under it, endurance has its perfect result. Like runners in a race, no matter how tired you get you keep on until the race is finished. And you do not break the rules by running across the infield to come in first. You stay in your lane and run according to the rules. When the race of a "trial" has been endured, the result will be a person who is perfect, complete, lacking in nothing.

To be perfect is to be mature and of full age. This word in the Greek has the idea of goodness. The Lord wants us to become more and more like Him, for we are told in Romans 8:29 that God has predestined us to be conformed to His image. He has marked out our course, He has planned our lives. Therefore the trials that come into our lives have been left there by the Lord to cause us to become more like Him. Our job is to go through our trials in a way that is pleasing to God. If we will respond to trials the way the Lord would, we will find out that His ways work. To discover this — and to later respond according to His ways again because we *know* it works — is maturity, and we become more like Him.

By persevering we not only mature, but we are told that we become complete. This means we will be perfectly sound, someone who can be depended upon. We can be depended upon because the dross in us, as in silver that is being refined, will be burned off, leaving the good behind. Did you know that when silver has been refined often enough, it never has to be polished? So, when we have learned all that God wants us to do in an area, we might not be tested in that area again. The trouble is, we don't catch on and have to relearn so many things!

There are many times when we think we don't know what we are supposed to do in a trial. We are told in James 1 to ask God for wisdom and are promised that He will give to us generously, without bawling us out for asking. But note that we must ask in faith, without doubting, because one who doubts is like the surf of the sea driven and tossed by the wind. We must not expect to receive anything from the Lord if we are double-minded. One who is double-minded is unstable in all his ways.

In James 4:1-3, the Lord says,

> What is the source of quarrels and conflicts among you? Is not the source your pleasures that wage war in your members? You lust and do not have; so you commit murder. And you are envious and cannot obtain; so you fight and quarrel. You do not have because you do not ask. You ask and do not receive because you ask with wrong motives, so that you may spend it on your pleasures.

We talk to the Lord and say we want His way, and yet we are not willing to live like He wants us to. We want answers to our prayers, and yet when we pray we pray with the wrong motives. We want our own way, for our own pleasure. We forget so quickly that God wants us to put the interests of others before our own. Wanting our own way, while professing to want the Lord's way, makes us double-minded and unstable. We get confused and do not know which way to go, for our minds and hearts are not fully on serving the Lord. God will not give wisdom to someone who hasn't decided to fully follow Him. He wants our complete commitment. He wants us to regard Him and His way as our only treasure. He has told us in Matthew 6:19-21,

> Do not lay up for yourselves treasures upon earth, where moth and rust destroy, and where thieves break in and steal; but lay up for yourselves treasures in heaven, where neither moth nor rust destroys, and where thieves do not break in or steal; for where your treasure is, there will your heart be also.

As I've mentioned, in Scripture the terms *heart* and *mind* are interchangeable. What we think about and dwell on can be said to be in our hearts or in our minds. Our problem is that we have not decided to continually put the Lord first in our hearts and our minds. Many of us have decided to put ourselves first. Then we get upset with God because we do not think He hears our prayers. He hears, but He has set up conditions that He wants us to follow before His answers come. The question we need to ask God is not "Why?" but "How?" How does He want me to go through this trial?

We already see an answer to "Why?" in 1 Corinthians 1:3-5.

> Blessed be the God and Father of our Lord Jesus Christ, the Father of mercies, and God of all comfort, who comforts us in all our affliction so that we may be able to comfort those who are in any affliction with the comfort with which we ourselves are comforted by God. For just as the sufferings of Christ are ours in abundance, so also our comfort is abundant through Christ.

To comfort someone means to make him strong. As we go through a trial in a God-honoring way, doing it His way, we are comforted and made strong by God. In return, we can then comfort others with the same comfort God has given us. God wants us to use our lives to minister to others. We must look at each trial in our lives and think how we can use it for "ministering currency."

The comfort we offer will be real, because others will know we have come through the same kind of trials they are now experiencing. We can comfort them wisely because we can tell them about our obedience to the Lord and how He worked out our problems for us.

It's a fact that we WILL have trials and we WILL suffer. Jesus Christ told us a slave is not greater than his master. If Jesus Christ suffered, then we can expect to suffer also. And we encourage others when they see us go through trials in a godly way — a different way than that of people who don't know the Lord. It is wonderful and special to see a person go through trials with serenity because he or she trusts God.

I've watched my mother go through life with a lovely, serene attitude because her trust was in the Lord. My brothers and I were born just before and during the Depression. Dad always had a job, but the pay was small. When we were very young Mother picked cherries, and also worked in the apple orchards to help pollinate blossoms and then thinning the apples after they "set on." She took us kids with her to "help." After we started attending school, she packed cherries, peaches, pears and apples. Sometimes she would work ten- and twelve-hour days.

When the "working" day was over, she would preserve and can fruit and vegetables — quarts and quarts. Of course we would all help her, including Dad, but she had the greatest burden. Mom never complained, nor did we even know she was doing anything extraordinary.

The folks raised a garden for fresh vegetables, chickens for eggs, rabbits and a pig for meat, and a goat for milk. Mom and Dad were so matter-of-fact about this kind of life that we thought this was what everyone did. We enjoyed each other and had so much fun together that we didn't know we were poor. We did notice, however, that we had more work to do than our friends.

This certainly was a trial for both Mom and Dad, but because of their acceptance of the situation we kids were peaceful and secure. We learned so much through those experiences, and it has helped us in our marriages and in raising our children.

Remember that the apostle Paul said he had to LEARN how to be content with little. He said in Philippians 4:12-13,

> I know how to get along with humble means, and I also know how to live in prosperity; in any and every circumstance I have learned the secret of being filled and going hungry, both of having abundance and suffering need. I can do all things through Him who strengthens me.

Because my brothers are older than I, I asked them to tell me some of the things they remember about our family when we were learning to live on little. They remember going fishing together as a family "for fun," but realize now it was for food, because Mom would pack the fish in salt for winter use. They remember making soap from pig fat, and applesauce in July from apples that wouldn't be ready for market until September. They remember lots and lots of oatmeal and the delicious brown-sugar refrigerator cookies for breakfast. On bread-baking day we had "fried bread" (still one of our favorite meals) for lunch with butter and homemade jam or jelly. They remember getting a load of scrap lumber with odds and ends to build toys. They thought it was especially for them, but it was really fuel for the cook stove.

I remember making dresses out of calico flour sacks, and straight wool skirts out of discarded men's trousers. And it seemed Mom could make a meal out of anything. If we were out of potatoes we put gravy on bread. When we were out of something, we did without until we had money to buy more (there were no credit cards in those days). We didn't fill up on meat, for our pieces of meat were allotted. But we were never hungry because we had Mom's good homemade bread.

When we became teenagers we worked in the summers. My brothers made apple boxes because our uncle bought a semi-automatic box maker so they would have a job. I packed fruit alongside Mom. Later she became my boss, and made sure I did a good job. We used the money we earned to buy our school clothes and to put away for our college education. I learned to work no matter how tired I was, because when fruit is ready it will not wait. We learned the same principle while raising animals — they always need care.

Apples were harvested about the time school started each year, so when I was in the seventh grade I began taking over the family shopping and cooking while Mother packed apples. This was before meat was prepackaged. I was always embarrassed to tell the meat-men what I wanted because I thought they were laughing at me. Now I know they were amused only because I was so young. During this time Mom taught me to have the table set for supper no matter how far along I was in preparing it. She told me that as long as Dad saw the table set, he knew supper would soon be ready.

Like Paul in Philippians, we "learned" how to live contentedly in hard times. And we learned the most by seeing Dad and Mom's example and attitude. We are better able to cope with hard circumstances now because we are trying to follow their example.

We need people today like my parents who go through trials in such a God-honoring way. We need single-minded people, doing only those things that are pleasing to the Lord.

The promise of blessing is ours when we keep on persevering. "For once he has been approved, he will receive the crown of life, which the Lord has promised to those who love Him" (James 1:12). We have honored my parents because they persevered for us. We hold them in high esteem because of how they handled their trials. The Lord has blessed them not only with a fine family, but also with a family that cares for them, as they cared for us. Dad is in heaven now, and Mom keeps on persevering as always. She is the cutest, most sparkling great-grandmother in Wenatchee, Washington. The Lord's light shines brightly through her.

On the other hand, we can turn a trial into a temptation. Temptations lead us astray. When we are tempted, we are being led to fail. Temptation is the opposite of a *trial,* which is a test to bring about good. Temptations come from our fleshly desires, from worldly enticements or from Satan himself. We see this explained in James 4:1-7. And we know that God does not tempt us to evil, for James 1:13 states, "Let no one say when he is tempted, 'I am being tempted by God'; for God cannot be tempted by evil, and He Himself does not tempt anyone."

The reason we have to be so single-minded in putting the Lord first is that temptation comes when we are carried away and enticed by our own lusts. Even though we are tempted by the world or Satan, the flesh is always the entryway for sin. The word *lust* does not always mean sexual lust. We lust or have a passion or strong desire for recognition, for riches, for friends, for power, for influence, for relationships, for our own way, and on and on. Our wants and desires (lusts) may get in the way of our commitment to the Lord. However, if we are not double-minded it is not as apt to happen.

Professional football players and baseball players are not double-minded. They have a goal to be a great player. When given the temptation of over-eating or not doing their conditioning exercises, they know exactly what they have to do. After all, it is their livelihood that is at stake.

Well, *our* livelihood is at stake too when we face temptation. Our well-being is in the Lord — our peace, our maturity, our blessings from the Lord. We often put our wants before the Lord and do not even recognize the consequences when they come.

The things that will tempt YOU may not even phase me, and vice versa. We need to know ourselves and stay away from those things or situations that will get to us.

Since I am expressive, I have to guard my mouth all the time. I have to pray and ask God to put a seal on my mouth. I have to keep my thoughts in control, for if I don't, sure enough out pops the wrong thing. I have been tempted and given in, but I have also been able to turn temptation into a trial and come out of it more mature because of obedience. Maturity is achieved when one obeys, sees the good results of the obedience, and says to one's self, "I'm going to obey again, because when I do, not only do I stay out of trouble, but I'm blessed by the Lord."

You see, "When lust has conceived, it gives birth to sin; and when sin is accomplished, it brings forth death." This is death in some form or another to relationships, or to innocence, or to purity, or even to the knowledge that you have God's approval. When you love someone, you do not want to displease him; and when you do displease him, something dies in you.

The Lord says, "Submit therefore to God. Resist the devil and he will flee from you. Draw near to God and He will draw near to you" (James 4:7-8). We draw near to God by obedience. When we are of full age, after having gone through many temptations and trials, we resist temptations much more readily knowing that unpleasant consequences will come if we don't. Consequences always come, one way or another. I want

the consequences for my actions to be blessings rather than
disapproval from God.

So — the choice. When Chuck and I disagree, what do we
do? Because we've chosen wrongly so many times through the
past thirty-four years, we are more careful now. We have expe-
rienced the result of obedience, which is a loving relationship
and a blessing, and also the result of sin. We have considered
the results of each and have chosen to follow the Lord and
walk in His way.

Who cares, really, if the baggage or the car is picked up
first at the airport? And why would I want Chuck to eat anything he does not enjoy? And why not take *his* favorite way
across the mountains instead of mine? I happened to have the
first insight about how unhappy Chuck was when he was stuck
driving behind slow traffic on the narrower road I like best. So
when setting out for the trip, I learned to pick his way when he
asked which way I wanted to go. Of course, now he knows
which is MY favorite way, and it's hard to get him to go his
way anymore.

When I'm driving he does not insist on shortcuts, and
when he's driving I let him take all the shortcuts he wants. He
himself will not send back food in a restaurant, but he lets me
be me, and I can send back an undercooked steak without his
disapproval.

Chuck and I saw a sign once that said, "Don't sweat the
little things." That helped us so much at the time. Later, in a
book on anger titled *Is It Worth Dying For?*, Chuck ran across
the more complete quote: "Don't sweat the little things. They
are all little things."

My way of standing by my man is to let him be himself. He
treats me the same way. And because we do, we are regarding
one another as more important than ourselves (Philippians

2:3). We've had our trials with each other and continue to do so, even to this day. But our goal is to walk pleasing to God, and therefore we get over the trials sooner and try not to turn them into temptations.

Remember, maturity is handling your trials in a God-honoring way, and then getting over your differences quickly. It doesn't mean not having any differences at all. Different opinions will always be with us, but the choice is ours. Will we keep them a trial, or turn them into temptation? We've found trials to be easier in the long run because when we persevere through the trial in a God-honoring way, the Lord teaches us and causes growth in us.

Sometimes I just hate it when Chuck and I always seem to have different opinions. I know he feels the same way. But no matter who we married, the same thing would happen.

We're different. And it's okay.

THOUGHTS TO CONSIDER

Do you regard others as more important than yourself, or are you selfish?

Have you decided to look out for the interests of others because God wants you too, not because you want something from them?

When you are in a trial, do you ask God HOW He wants you to go through it?

Do you ask for God's wisdom to walk through your trial in a God-honoring way?

Are you more concerned with WHY you're going through the trial than HOW you'll go through it?

Do you know that God promises blessing if you go through your trial in a God-honoring way?

Is your goal to "walk pleasing to Him"?

Where is your heart — storing up heavenly treasure, or storing up treasure on earth?

Remember: When you handle your trials the way the Lord would, you will be a blessing to others. He will use you to minister to and comfort others the way He has comforted you.

Do you want the Lord's way more than you want your own?

SCRIPTURES TO KNOW

1 PETER 3:8-9
To sum up, let all be harmonious, sympathetic, brotherly, kindhearted, and humble in spirit; not returning evil for evil, or insult for insult, but giving a blessing instead; for you were called for the very purpose that you might inherit a blessing.

JAMES 1:2-5
Count it all joy, my brethren, when you encounter various trials; knowing that the testing of your faith produces endurance. And let endurance have its perfect result, that you may be perfect and complete, lacking in nothing. But if any of you lacks wisdom, let him ask of God, who gives to all men generously and without reproach, and it will be given to him.

JAMES 1:12
Blessed is a man who perseveres under trial; for once he has been approved, he will receive the crown of life, which the Lord has promised to those who love Him.

MATTHEW 6:19-21
Do not [as a habit of life] lay up for yourselves treasures upon earth, where moth and rust destroy, and where thieves break in and steal; but lay up for yourselves treasures in heaven, where neither moth nor rust destroys, and where thieves do not break in or steal; for where your treasure is, there will your heart be also.

HIS *HOME* & MINE

> ...so that He may establish your hearts
> unblamable in holiness before our God and Father
> at the coming of our Lord....
> 1 THESSALONIANS 3:13

WHEN WE DROVE from Washington state to New Jersey to start two years of Army service, it took us fifteen days. Chuck said we knew every service station attendant from here to there because by that time I was already five months pregnant. At each station we stopped at I had to get the restroom key from the front office, so I became acquainted with many people.

We took along an electric frying pan and a cooler so we could rent a kitchenette and cook for ourselves and save money. We had some interesting times cooking and washing dishes when we couldn't find a motel that had rooms with a kitchen.

When we arrived for our three months in New Jersey we rented an apartment just one block from the Atlantic Ocean. I had not yet seen even the Pacific Ocean, despite living within easy driving distance of it all my life.

We moved three times in the next year. After going from New Jersey to North Carolina we rented a home not far from Fort Bragg. We soon tired of commuting, and moved onto the base. We lived in an old converted hospital barracks. All our furniture was army issue, and included only cots, tables and chairs, and desks. Nothing pretty or soft. We made a home-made couch by taking the ends off a metal army bed, putting new wooden legs on the frame, rolling a mattress for the back-rest, and covering it all with a melon-colored denim. It looked quite pretty for what it was. We bought a padded rocker with wooden arms for $12 and I covered it in a melon, cream, and blue striped denim that complemented the couch. Mom sent a check so I could buy a lifetime membership in my college sorority, but instead I bought some nylon priscilla curtains for the windows.

That was the extent of our furnishings. We thought it was charming.

We soon moved to "Wherry Housing," which was much nicer, with hardwood floors. I knew so little about how to care for them that I used to drench them with water and mop them like any kitchen floor, before putting on paste wax. We had no carpeting, so I had to keep them extra clean. It was years before I found out this was the wrong way to clean wood floors.

We could not have army issue furniture in Wherry Hous-ing, so as soon as we could we bought a table and chair set. Chuck picked it out because he liked the woodgrain formica and the wrought-iron legs. We bought a double bed for us; we already had a bed for Tim, and I used apple boxes to hold our clothes. I set them up like shelves, and they were handy. But we wanted so much to have dressers, so we bought two for $10 each at the base second-hand store, and painted them to "match." We used those dressers until last year, when Chuck built us a pine armoire, a pine dresser with mirror, and a pine trunk. This is the first time in our married life that we have a truly matching bedroom set.

Chuck was always busy back then too. He insisted that he needed a workshop, so Tim had to share his room with his Dad. Chuck bought a second-hand steel workbench and placed it at one end of Tim's room. Most nights Chuck would go in and out of the room several times to work at his bench. Whenever he did this, Tim would awaken from a sound sleep, stand up and watch, and then go back to sleep when his Dad left. It didn't seem to matter to Tim at all.

I can't remember everything Chuck did in his workshop, but I do remember that he had a coin collection, and he drew every map he could of Civil War battlefields. If we had ten minutes before we had an appointment, Chuck would work on a project during that time. Even if he had only five minutes he would use them to accomplish something. When I had time to spare, I would just relax.

Chuck bought me a Pfaff sewing machine shortly after we were married, and I made all of Tim's clothes. I wouldn't put him in a T-shirt for I didn't have a dryer, and they didn't dry in shape. I made him little cotton shirts that cost us less than thirty-nine cents — fabric was thirty-nine cents a yard, and I needed less than a yard to make the shirt. These had to be starched and ironed, for that's what we did in those days. I ironed all of Chuck's uniforms, which were heavily starched also.

After living with our folks for about five months while getting resettled in Seattle after our Army days, we rented a home when Chuck started working at KING-TV. This is where we first knew that we did not decorate houses the same. I wanted to have all the walls off-white, and he wanted COLOR! I wanted color also, but not on the walls; I wanted color in the furniture and accessories. But since we did not know that a woman's personality should be expressed in how her home is decorated, just as a man's personality is expressed in his work and career, I let Chuck have his colors. (I was supposed to be submissive, wasn't I?!) He picked spring colors for each room. The house had one main living-dining room, and every other room opened off of it. We had bright spring gold in the living-dining room, bright spring pink in one bedroom, bright blue in the bath and kitchen, and apple green in the other bedroom. I picked white for the woodwork. We did the painting ourselves, for we were able to work off some rent that way.

We lived in our brightly colored house until we had been married seven years. Then my dad told us if we wanted to buy a house, he would loan us money for the down-payment. At first Chuck declined, but within two weeks we were out looking.

We found what we thought was the perfect house. We prayed about it and asked the Lord for peace if we were to buy it. When we went back to see it again we felt no peace. So we went home to think about it. Still no peace. But, WE decided that it was such a good deal we could not pass it up. So we made an offer. Another offer had been made, so we countered. Then our real estate agent told us that when he presented our counter offer, the other party agreed to pay cash.

We felt spanked. How many people can pay cash for a house? We knew the Lord had protected us, but why? We soon found out.

We found another house, one that had been sold to someone who later could not get financing. When we stepped onto the porch of this "dream home," the sold sign was just then being taken down. The next day, our agent put another one up. We were the proud owners of the most beautiful two-story

Colonial we had ever seen. The lot was more than twice the size of other lots on the street, and the house was spacious. There was a lot of fix-up work to do, but we were glad to do it.

We scraped off wallpaper and painted. Chuck stripped off the old finish on the kitchen cupboards and refinished them one by one. We put cream-colored formica on the twenty-one feet of counter space. We bought our first matching couch and chair (which we continue to use, twenty-five years later). My mother gave us muslin priscilla curtains.

The house was beautiful, except for one thing: the carpet. It was laid wall to wall, but was all cotton. It had once been a lovely champagne color, but now it had gun-metal gray walk-ways through it. I bought every cleansing solution known to man, wet and dry, and used every cleaning machine I could to try to clean that rug. I planned and looked and planned and looked for a new carpet, and we saved up money for it. But each time I thought we could buy it, Chuck would instead buy another piece of equipment that he "just had to have" for his business (by now he had his own advertising agency).

I knew that the business supplied our needs, but I sometimes wondered if everything Chuck wanted was really "needed" in the way I NEEDED a new carpet. Chuck had divided our "wish" lists into wants and needs, and it went this way: He *needs* a new camera for the agency, I *want* a new rug; he *needs* new sound equipment, I *want* something else for the house. You can see how it worked. Chuck thought it worked so well that I waited NINE years to get that new carpet. When he finally realized how much a new carpet would mean to me, he let me carpet both upstairs and down. I've always liked one carpet color running through the whole house, so this was beautiful to me — a dream come true!

In those days greens were in vogue, and I picked out a

beautiful green that did not show dirt. It did not show dog stains (I know, because our dog Molly initiated it the first day, right in the middle of the dining room). That carpet looked as good the day we sold the house seven years later as it did the day we put it in.

Our children were raised in that home. We had moved there when Tim was six and Bev was four, and they were college-age when we sold it. It was as hard for them to move as it was for me.

When we did move, we moved because Chuck had another idea! He wanted to have a home that would more easily lend itself to hospitality. We had accommodated overnight guests many times through the years, but Chuck thought they needed private bedrooms with their own baths, etc.

About that time we were given a trip to Hawaii. As we were having a moonlit dinner on a long, beautiful porch, with music and the sound of lapping waves close by, we dreamed about being able to have a large, comfortable house that we could share with visiting friends. We'd had many missionaries stay with us over the years, and we thought it would be such a treat if we could provide them with some place nice to stay.

So Chuck prayed for the house without asking me exactly what kind of home I wanted. Without consulting me, he prayed for a spiral staircase. (I prefer a more informal feel.) He prayed to be close to the city with a view of the mountains. He prayed for a room for an audio studio, and land for a tennis court.

Chuck prayed these things while driving to a business meeting. Before he returned to the office, a friend who sells houses called and told us he wanted to show us a place. When I heard how much it cost I knew we could never afford it —

and besides, I didn't want to move. But I did want to see what a house in this price range looked like, so we went to view it.

The house was in the middle of the city, but was set on a wooded, four-acre plot. We drove down a lane lined by trees, past a lighted tennis court, then past a swimming pool and pool house, and reached a circle drive surrounding a small pool and fountain. The house was brick, with a beautiful entryway.

As we toured the house, Chuck got more excited by the moment. And I had the strangest feeling that the Lord was telling me this would be our home. *But Lord,* I was saying, *we can't afford it, and I don't really want to move. Anyway, we haven't seen a room for the audio studio yet.*

When we finished seeing the main part of the house, we toured the basement.. We opened one door into a film studio, and the next door led to a long room just right to be converted into an audio studio.

It had taken us years to paint and redecorate our other home and get it just the way I wanted it. Now, at this stage in my life, I felt I did not have the energy to decorate another home. But — as the Lord would have it — we moved into the big house in the four-acre woods on September 1, 1977.

This house has twenty-seven rooms, including six bathrooms and seven bedrooms. Our living room is so large that we had to buy four couches for it. Little by little we have filled up the whole house with furniture and memories.

One day our children were trying to decide what things in the house they wanted for themselves if we were to die. The living room couches weren't taken, for they did not have enough memories for them. It was fun to hear what was important to them. (I'll tell you about our children in the next chapter.)

Chuck let me decorate our new home. (The only thing he did was tell me what a good job I was doing!) Because the house is so large, I asked a friend who is an interior decorator to help me decorate. He hired a wonderful gal to assist him. We worked well together, and yet I felt I needed to make this place my own. They understood. So through them I ordered the living room furniture, new wood floors, new carpet and wall-fabric for the dining room, and wallpaper for the kitchen, while I purchased the rest myself.

This house, too, has taken years to become what I wanted, but people say they feel it is warm and cozy here. I feel really at home here now, and it's beautiful — but it's almost too big, and it's built so well that you can't hear from room to room. I've been known to lock Chuck in the basement before I go to bed because I think he's already upstairs. One night he set off the security alarm off because I turned it on without realizing he was in the studio downstairs. Another time he was in the house for about an hour, and I kept taking phone messages for him because I didn't know he was home. Now we report in to each other so we know where we are.

Though I have been allowed to decorate, our home DOES express both of us. Chuck has an office in a former bedroom in the basement, and he has made it into a museum of memories. It's filled with pictures and souvenirs and antiques that he loves. I had it wallpapered in a design he likes, and he's done the rest. He also claimed the large furnace room in the basement, except for one corner where I have the washer and dryer. He has the film studio, which is now his computer room, and of course the audio studio. He has a rolltop desk and file-cabinet in an upstairs bedroom where I also have a desk and files. He has the triple garage outfitted with his woodworking tools. And he has built an exercise house out by the garage (which contains a universal gym which he bought on impulse, then discovered was too tall to fit in the basement; besides, he says the addition will "up the resale of the property, don't you know?"). Chuck has also put in horseshoe pits and a sport court. So far I've been able to resist his putting a "lid" on the tennis court and adding an ice-cream parlor/video room to the basement.

I do not ask Chuck to keep his areas mess-free on a day-to-day basis, but when we have company, without a word from me, he cleans them up, for our visitors always want a tour.

Remember when the Lord said He was going away to prepare a home for us? Since He is our example, I also want to have a prepared home for my family. No matter where we have lived, I have always tried to have our home a place where Chuck and our children could be nurtured in peace and serenity. I've always tried to have the refrigerator and cupboards full of food that they enjoy. I've tried to keep clean clothes in the drawers, and to keep the ironing done. In fact, when the children were young I washed on Mondays, ironed on Tuesdays, cleaned on Thursdays, and shopped for groceries on Friday. I sewed on any day. Saturdays and Sundays were just for feeding and caring for the family, and having fun. I think this was as it should be; it worked for us, and that's why I think it is good. The Lord made me the guardian of the home — the keeper at home — and it kept me very busy, even when the children were in school. It takes time and energy to have everything "prepared" for the family.

A fond memory of ours is having dinner together at 6:00 each evening. I know that children are playing sports and involved in many other activities now, but our kids were not. Dinner time together was a special time to talk, to have well-balanced meals, and to get to know each other better. I can remember when Bev was four and had not yet prayed out loud at the dinner table. Chuck asked her one night to pray, and she shyly refused. Chuck said, "Please, Bev. The Lord hasn't heard from you since you've been here!" When she finally did start praying, we could not shut her down — she went on and on.

Along with telling us in Titus to love our husbands and our children, the Lord also tells us to be kind and subject to our own husbands so the Word of God will not be dishonored (Titus 2:3-5). When we take on too much, as I've said before, we start thinking, *Why does the Lord expect so much from me?* But WE are the ones who have decided to do too much. When we blame it on the Lord, our attitude dishonors Him. We have used most of our energy outside the home, and it is hard to give more energy to all the demands that we naturally have as a wife and mother. As I said before, I do *not* believe women are prohibited in Scripture from working outside the home; after all, the Proverbs 31 commends a woman who is doing just that. But I do believe we can put too much of a burden on ourselves when we do.

Being loving and kind are the first things to go when we are so tired. And isn't it love that "makes the world go round"? We don't have the energy or time to have chocolate chip cookies hot from the oven when the kids get home from school, or to make homemade bread, or to just be there to listen. Again, I'd opt for home and memory-making any day. It takes time to "be."

I learned to walk through the house before going to bed, making sure everything is picked up, put away, and in place. It makes it so much easier to get up in the morning, for it takes away the feeling of confusion and "too much to do." During the day I had to learn to limit how much time I spent on the phone. The phone can be a robber of precious time, and when you get behind, you become irritable easier. If I were young again, I would read about time management, especially in the home.

Here's a list of things that our homes should be, from a biblical viewpoint. These Scriptures show what God does for us, what He is like, and the pattern He has set for us.

The home should be prepared.

> ...for I go and prepare a place for you. (John 14:2)

Our homes should be righteous, joyful, and peaceful.

> For the kingdom of God is not eating and drinking, but righteousness and peace and joy in the Holy Spirit. (John 14:2)

Our homes should have no unclean thing in them. They should be holy, set apart for God's use only.

> And I saw the holy city, new Jerusalem, coming down out of heaven from God, made ready as a bride adorned for her husband....And nothing unclean and no one who practices abomination and lying, shall ever come into it, but only those whose names are written in the Lamb's book of life. (Revelation 21:2,27)

Our homes should be a place for teaching God's ways.

> Thou wilt make known to me the path of life;
> In Thy presence is fullness of joy;
> In Thy right hand there are pleasures forever. (Psalm 16:11)

Our homes should be a place of committed, initiating love.

The Lord appeared to him from afar, saying,
"I have loved you with an everlasting love;
Therefore I have drawn you with lovingkindness.
(Jeremiah 31:3)

In this is love, not that we loved God, but He loved us and sent His son to be the propitiation for our sins. (1 John 4:10)

We love because He first loved us. If someone says, "I love God," and hates his brother he is a liar; for the one who does not love his brother whom he has seen, cannot love God whom he has not seen. (1 John 4:19-20)

Our homes should give one another security and total acceptance.

What then shall we say to these things? If God is for us, who is against us? (Romans 8:31)

Let your way of life be free from the love of money, being content with what you have; for He Himself has said, "I will never desert you, nor will I ever forsake you." So that we confidently say, "The Lord is my helper, I will not be afraid. What shall man do to me?" (Hebrews 13:5-6)

There should be loving discipline in our homes.

It is for discipline that you endure; God deals with you as with sons; for what son is there whom his father does not discipline? But if you are without discipline, of which all have become partakers, then you are illegitimate children and not sons. (Hebrews 12:7-8)

And our homes should be a place where parents give good gifts to their children.

If you then, being evil, know how to give good gifts to your children, how much more shall your Father who is in heaven give what is good to those who ask Him? Therefore, whatever you want others to do for you, do so for them; for this is the Law and the Prophets. (Matthew 7:11-12)

Let me review. We are to have a prepared home, one that is prepared not only physically, but also spiritually, where righteousness, peace, and joy dwell. We are to love our children and each other with an unconditional love. This kind of love makes our families feel accepted and secure. We must give our children proper instruction and training. Instruction is verbal, and training is by example. And we are to discipline our children for the purpose of righteousness and holiness. Holiness means being set apart for His use only.

If we would carry out all these instructions, our children would love it, our husband would adore us, and we would be women who are content. We would have approval from God and from our families.

We are so shortsighted when it comes to obeying all that we are instructed. As Lawrence O. Richards says, "God's call to obedience is a loving invitation to experience His best."

In response to God's best for us, Chuck feels our home is a place where he can love his family and "do" things with them in order to show his love. For me, it's a place where I can love my family and "be" a godly woman — loving my family in such a tender way that they will feel God's love through me.

So once again we see Chuck into "doing" and goals, and me into relationships and "being." And yet, even in our difference we ultimately have the same purpose: to establish the hearts of our family so they will be unblamable in holiness before our God and Father at the coming of our Lord (1 Thessalonians 3:13).

THOUGHTS TO CONSIDER

Is your home a prepared place for your family?

Is your home righteous? Joyful? Peaceful? Pure — set apart for God?

Is it a place where God's ways are taught?

Are you completely committed to your family, or mostly to yourself?

Do you initiate love in your home by doing kind, thoughtful deeds, and speaking to build others up?

Does your family feel totally accepted and secure in your presence?

Do you understand that you are not raising children, but men and women?

Is your discipline consistent and loving — not done in anger?

Are you giving to your family, or do you take from them?

Is your desire to present your family and yourself blameless at the coming of our Lord and Savior Jesus Christ?

SCRIPTURES TO KNOW

PHILIPPIANS 2:3-5

Do nothing from selfishness or empty conceit, but with humility of mind let each of you regard one another as more important than himself; do not merely look out for your own personal interest, but also for the interests of others. Have this attitude in yourselves which was also in Christ Jesus.

PHILIPPIANS 2:14-16

Do all things without grumbling or disputing; that you may prove yourselves to be blameless and innocent, children of God above reproach in the midst of a crooked and perverse generation, among whom you appear as lights in the world, holding fast the word of life....

And you shall love the LORD your God with all your heart
and with all your soul and with all your might. And these words,
which I am commanding you today, shall be on your heart; and you
shall teach them diligently to your sons and shall talk of them
when you sit in your house and when you walk by the way
and when you lie down and when you rise up.
DEUTERONOMY 6:5-7

TEN MONTHS AND FOUR DAYS — that's how long it took
the two of us to become three. Our son Tim was born on
December 10, 1955, at Fort Monmouth, New Jersey. My labor
started thirty hours before he was born.

In those days, especially in the Army, we had no childbirth
classes, so I didn't really know what to expect. When I thought
labor had started I ran upstairs to a neighbor and explained my
symptoms. She assured me that I was, in fact, starting labor.

We had planned to have a gathering at our house that
night to play games, and we went ahead with it. At midnight
we decided we should go to the hospital. When we drove up
to the gate, Chuck informed the guard why we were there. As I

remember, Chuck saluted him many more times than he needed to. When I was settled in the hospital room, Chuck had to leave, for they did not allow fathers-to-be to stay. I heard the phone ring often though, and the nurse usually came and told me it was Chuck.

My mother was coming by train. This was her first time to travel alone. When she arrived in Newark, we had her paged and asked her to catch another train to Long Branch. We were young, and thought it was more important for Chuck to stay by the phone than going to pick up Mother. Now I just mourn to think of her arriving from her cross-country trip expecting to be met by us, and being met only by a phone call asking her to catch another train. How could we do that to her? She was brave, though, and did as we asked. She arrived in time for Tim's birth at 9:00 that night.

She stayed with us for three weeks. When she left I asked her what I was to do when Tim cried. She said, "Just hold him."

It was frightening to be alone, all the way across the United States from our families, but we soon got into the swing of it and enjoyed Tim more than we can say. But we missed sharing him with grandparents, aunts, uncles, and cousins.

We planned to have our children eighteen months apart, but the Lord had other plans. A miscarriage at two months brought sorrow to us. Then we kept telling each other, "We can't get pregnant now" since the baby would be born just as Chuck was leaving the Army. But Beverly Anne was born the day before Chuck was discharged. So much for planning.

Because of Bev's due date, Tim and I came home to Washington two months earlier than Chuck, because in those days they did not let pregnant women fly after their seventh month.

We settled in at my parents' home. My brother Phil was studying to be a doctor and had to do military service that summer, so his wife Maxine and two children were also living there. Our poor folks! They had three grandchildren, a daughter, and a daughter-in-law living with them for the whole summer. Of course, Mom still worked with fruit, but she had us canning fruit and vegetables and making pickles and jam until the harvest was over. I don't know how we found enough jars to preserve as much as we did.

When Bev was eleven days old, Chuck and I drove to Tacoma to live with his folks, so he could begin job hunting in Seattle. She was five months old when Chuck started work at KING-TV.

Tim, as a toddler, was obedient, quiet, and cuddly. When Bev arrived he wanted attention and started doing everything he could to get it.

Bev wasn't like her brother. Tim would sleep anywhere — even in a crowded room or a bowling alley — but Bev cried and took constant attention. Tim as a preschooler was easy to raise, but Bev had a mind of her own and knew she was right. (We thought we had trained Tim so well, but now learned it wasn't our training that made him so compliant.)

Just before Tim started school, I remember saying, "I don't know what I'm going to do with Bev. I just can't control her in stores, and I need Tim to keep her out of trouble!" But after Tim was in school, Bev was just wonderful when we went shopping. She obeyed me, too. All she needed was more personal attention from me.

We talked a lot about the Lord in our family, and we all went to Sunday school and church every week. We read to them, or at least tried, for they were each trying to turn the pages, and you know how that goes. I wish I had spent more time reading to them, instead of stopping because they were arguing. I did not know enough about age characteristics. I should have just put up with it. That's one of the things that is so wonderful for young parents now. They have so much written for them to help them understand their children. When I went to the library when Tim was about ten years old, there was only one book on the shelf about age characteristics.

But there was another book written centuries ago that is the best ever written on child development — the Bible. Years later I studied what the Bible said about raising children, and wished I had known it before.

Here are some principles from Deuteronomy 6-7, with other cross-references noted:

Parents are to obey God first by the way they live.
Matthew 6:33 tells us to seek first His kingdom and His righteousness. Our obedience is to be a way of life that our children will see. Deuteronomy 6:7 tells us that we parents are to teach our children when we...
> walk by the way.
> sit at home.
> lie down.
> rise up.

WE are to be all that Jesus Christ wants THEM to be. They will then see us and imitate us, as we imitate God. Scripture tells us to be imitators of God, as beloved children; and to walk in love, just as Christ also loved us and gave Himself up for us (Ephesians 5:1-2). Our life is to be lived for the Lord and for others — in this case, our children.

We are to teach our children...
> to obey. (Deuteronomy 6:1,17,24)
> to fear the Lord. (6:13)

to serve the Lord. (6:13)

to swear by His name. (6:13)

to not go after other gods. (6:14)

to not tempt God (6:16) — that is, to not disobey God just to see if He will do as He says. (7:10, and Colossians 3:25)

to diligently keep God's commandments. (6:17)

to do what is right and good in the sight of the Lord. (6:18)

our testimony — how God has delivered us from the bondage of sin (6:20-21), and that in keeping His commandments, the Lord has shown us what righteousness is. (6:25)

the wonders God has performed in our lives (6:22)

that we are to always fear the Lord (that is, to stand in awe of Him, and have a wholesome dread of ever displeasing Him); and that the reason for this *is for our own good* (6:24) — so that He can prosper us (6:2), for our survival (6:24), and for a long life (6:2, and 1 Peter 3:10, Proverbs 9:10-11, and Psalm 34:12-14).

to not marry unbelievers. (7:3)

to destroy idols — anything that puts God second. (7:5)

that God loves you because you are you. (7:8)

that God is faithful. (7:9)

that God is just, and there are consequences for disobedience. (7:10)

that God keeps His Word (7:12-13)

that obedience brings rewards. (7:12-13)

In many ways I think Chuck and I *did* teach our children these principles, but it would have been great to have them written down and before us all the time, so we could have checked ourselves out to see how we were doing.

Another thing we didn't know is our children's learning patterns. Bev fit easily into our family rules; Tim had a harder time. Bev loved school and did well. She followed the rules and I don't remember a time when she got into trouble at school. Her homework was done on time and she often received straight A's. I used to think if Bev had lived in the time when God picked a mother for Jesus, He might have picked her.

Bev told us later that she would just watch to see what Tim did to make us unhappy, and then wouldn't do it. She says she was not perfect, and her heart had not yet been changed. She just out-smarted us. She performed.

Tim was our creative child. He always had a better idea than the one we were proposing. And he would keep trying to change our minds until with exasperation we would say, "Just do it because *I said* to do it!"

Tim is artistic. He is sensitive in the wonderful sense of the word. He is an idea person. And he was bored with school. We didn't know this was because he was creative. We should have given him more understanding than we did, but instead we kept telling him what he should "do." He wanted to "be." When his counselor told him he would not graduate unless he passed his biology test, Tim read the book and received a "B." Later he told me he could read down the pages of that book in his mind. He has a photographic memory.

Because we spent so much time trying to get Tim to "do" his homework, and "do" all that we thought he should, we set up an adversarial relationship. Therefore he could control us by not "doing" what we wanted.

Of course, Chuck's and my relationship suffered because we did not agree on how to handle the situations we had with

Tim. I thought Chuck was too hard on Tim, and he thought I was too soft. Soon I found myself handling a lot of the decision-making by myself. I could not understand why Chuck had backed off. Then we heard a speaker say that when the wife takes over, the husband backs off because he does not want to fail. That is what had happened to us. I asked Chuck to forgive me for taking over, and asked him to help out again. He did.

Each of Tim's teachers told us what a wonderful boy he was. This statement was usually followed by their question, "But how do you motivate him?" We did not have enough knowledge to know how, but in the years since we see that we should have admired and built him up verbally, telling him how much he was loved and enjoyed. We should have released him to be himself. We needed to tell him sooner that he was the one in charge of who he was and who he would become, and that there were certain consequences he would have to pay if he did not do his homework, or obey other rules we had. Yet even that was up to him. He could choose the work and the rules, or else face the negative consequences.

We didn't "release" Tim until after he graduated from high school. We told him that we would always be there to support him and to give him advice and counsel, but he had to make his own decisions. We had controlled him too much and too long with our own ideas.

After releasing him I decided to love him unconditionally, no matter what he did. In raising him I had tried to get him to do what I thought was best, but the time for my doing that was now over. This was the best decision I ever made concerning our relationship. Communication opened up between us. We began talking till all hours after saying we were on our way to bed. You see, he didn't change as much as I did.

The first decision Tim made was to not go to a Bible college we wanted him to attend. He decided to attend a junior college and learn to be a diesel mechanic. He loved school for the first time, and received straight A's. He soon took a job repairing fishing vessels in Alaska, and became foreman before he was twenty-three.

Now he runs a repair shop for fishing vessels and other ships here in Seattle. He made a great decision to do and be what he wanted.

Bev decided to go to Bible college. After two years there, she attended a two-year training program with Precept Ministries in Chattanooga, Tennessee. She also worked in the office, and was in charge of shipping out Bible study workbooks that had been ordered.

In 1979 Bev and her dad decided it was time for her to come home. When she came she asked the Lord for a friend who loved Him as much as she did. She soon met Debbie Amble.

Deb's folks have both passed away. I started thinking we should adopt her, for we all need to belong — really belong. I told the Lord that I would not say anything, and that if this thought was from Him, He should keep it in my mind.

Two weeks later I told Chuck, and he was thrilled with the idea. We decided to talk with Tim and Bev about it first. Before we could, we were all eating breakfast out one morning, and Tim looked across at Deb and said, "Why don't you let us adopt you, Deb?" We knew then that this was the Lord's will.

We asked Deb to become part of our family on April 20, 1988, and the adoption was final on August 3. We gave her a heart-shaped locket with "Chosen" inscribed on the back, and those two dates. Because the Lord chose her for us, we have chosen her to be ours.

Deb is a Bible teacher and a basketball coach at a Christian school here in Seattle.

Tim is married to Tammie. She first trusted in the Lord because a dear friend told her about Jesus Christ. Then the friend called us and said, "Don't you think Tim and Tam would be just perfect for each other?" I did, and they did too. Now they have two daughters, Kjersten and Brooke.

I looked back in my prayer journal the other day and read how I had prayed for Tim's future wife. I asked God to prepare her to be perfectly suited to him — and that she would be a woman of God who would follow Him fully. God answers prayer.

Bev is office manager and her dad's assistant at the advertising agency. She does the bookkeeping, and also keeps track of our speaking schedule. She teaches a Precept Bible Study group each week, and is the Precept Ministries trainer and coordinator for the state of Washington.

Two and a half years ago Bev met David DeChand, a godly young man who is interested in Bible study as she is. They plan to be married this summer.

Tim and Tammie are active in their church where Tammie works with the Awana program and Tim with high school kids. He hasn't forgotten his struggles growing up, and has great understanding for that age group. Tim and Tammie also lead a fellowship group that meets in their home once a month.

Now — for our granddaughter Kjersten! She is a creative child like her dad...only, this time we understand. Chuck and I were talking about her just this morning, about how she needs someone to say yes rather than no, someone (like her grandfather) who does not have to set up lots of rules, and who will not be too busy for her.

Because of our many conversations about creative children, Tim and Tam also realize the unique times that will be theirs in raising "The World's Most Perfect First-born Granddaughter."

Brooke is now six months old. She's a happy baby with grandparents eagerly watching her develop. Already we realize she is "The World's Most Perfect Second-born Granddaughter."

Chuck says he did not spend enough time with Tim and Bev because he was "too busy" with things he thought were important. Now he understands that the children were more important, and he does not want to miss out this time around. We believe God gives us grandchildren so we will have another chance to do it right. Chuck says grandparents are to "sprinkle stardust" in their grandchildren's lives.

God has been faithful to us. We determined to try and raise our children to follow the Lord, and to walk the narrow way. In our determination to do the right thing, we made many mistakes...but God overruled them.

When Tim was a teenager I told him, "You are who you are, because you have decided to be that person." I believe we — not others — determine our own character. But today, with a twinkle in my eye, I tell him, "You've turned out so well — I think it's all my fault!"

Chuck and I "have no greater joy than this, to hear of [our] children walking in truth" (3 John 4).

THOUGHTS TO CONSIDER

Children will imitate you, whether you want them to or not.

Do you love the Lord your God with all your heart, and with all your soul, and with all your might?

Are His words continually on your heart?

Are you teaching them diligently to your children as you go about your daily tasks?

Are you a living example of obeying the Lord?

When your children remember you, will they say you followed the Lord fully?

Are you a student of your children? Do you know their learning styles?

Are you raising each child "according to their own bent," as Proverbs 22:6 says? Or do you expect each child to be the same?

Do you pray for your children?

Are you teaching your children that to fear the Lord is to hate evil?

SCRIPTURES TO KNOW

PROVERBS 16:20
He who gives attention to the word shall find good,
And blessed is he who trusts in the LORD.

PROVERBS 14:26
In the fear of the LORD there is strong confidence,
And his children will have refuge.

PROVERBS 10:29
The way of the LORD is a stronghold to the upright,
But ruin to the workers of iniquity.

PROVERBS 8:13
The fear of the LORD is to hate evil;
Pride and arrogance and the evil way,
And the perverted mouth, I hate.

PROVERBS 4:23
Watch over your heart with all diligence,
For from it flow the springs of life.

HIS *PLEASURES* & MINE

> Wherefore accept one another,
> just as Christ also accepted us
> to the glory of God.
> ROMANS 14:7

TENNIS, BASKETBALL, pickleball, football, baseball, wood-working, writing, music, counseling, reading, family — doing, doing, doing.

Reading, studying, teaching, having lunch with friends, hand-work, being home, cooking, watching baseball and football games, family gatherings — being, being, being.

Active versus passive. Involved versus watching. Goals versus relationships. Making things happen versus letting things happen. Doing versus being.

One time when Chuck and I had a disagreement, I told him I hadn't had a moment's rest since the day I met him. It's been one of his favorite stories to tell. But it's true! He always has a new idea, and it usually involves me.

Over the years we have loved to play tennis together. We realize tennis can strain a marriage, but it is one of our favorite things to do. The only time we really had trouble on the court was when Chuck "double poached"! He ran across the net and hit a beautiful volley. I moved to the other side, ready to hit the return. He did a U-turn and ran back across to get the next shot. I don't remember if he made it or not, but I can certainly remember that this strained our marriage.

We don't often play tennis any more. I've had trouble with my back, so tennis is just occasional now. We do play pickleball now and then. It's played on a sport court with short handled paddles and a whiffleball. It's great fun, for neither person can overpower the other. It's also not as strenuous as tennis.

Sometimes we take walks together. We enjoy that, but we need to be in better shape to really enjoy it.

As I now write, this is the Christmas season. I've been so excited because I decided to buy Chuck a treadmill. We've had a Schwinn Air-dyne bike in the house for exercise, but Chuck does not think it does enough for him. I reasoned that since walking is the best form of exercise, he would be thrilled with an automated treadmill. After extensive research and much measuring to see if it would fit in our family room, I still could not decide on the brand. I had all the brochures with specifications and prices. My quandary was whether to buy a wide one so we could swing our arms as we walk, or a narrower one with oak trim that would look prettier but perhaps not do as good a job.

Then, yesterday morning Chuck decided to go out to the exercise house. I thought it was odd that he would decide to work out after such a long time. When he came in, I just could not keep from telling him that I was going to buy him a treadmill.

He smiled sheepishly, and informed me that he had just bought one.

"THE WEEK BEFORE CHRISTMAS?" I replied. I didn't feel wonderful about it. And he didn't feel wonderful about it either when I told him about my plan. We were both blue.

We went out to inspect the new machine. It was an inexpensive one. The motor was much too loud to use in our family room. No one could walk and watch television at the same time. We were both disappointed that my surprise had been ruined.

Then it occurred to me that I was being selfish. I was more concerned with my joy of surprising him than with his joy of doing an exercise he liked. I apologized, and then we decided to buy the more expensive, quiet one for the family room. It's really a good thing we found out about Chuck buying the cheap one before I ordered his present, because now *he* has to pay for it. We nearly lost our happy home yesterday, but it turned out okay after all.

One of our favorite things to do together is going out for breakfast. Well, I guess going out for lunch and dinner too. But at breakfast we like to buy the morning paper and read it together. It's fun to share the news and talk it over, and to see what our friends in professional sports are doing. Because of our involvement as speakers and counselors in the Christian organization Pro-Athletes Outreach, we have friends in professional football, baseball, hockey, golf, and rodeo. So there is usually news of someone we know.

These times together are wonderful for talking things over and just getting involved in each other's world. When we are out, the phone does not ring and our time is not interrupted.

Chuck has an electronic Yamaha keyboard. He has always loved to sing, but is shy about singing in front of me. Therefore he goes down to his audio studio alone and plays and sings till he is content. Most often it is just before bedtime. He loves gospel and western music.

On the other hand, I like to listen to Bible study tapes. I like "words" better than music. I"d much rather listen to talk on the radio than music. We both love to watch sporting events together. We go to at least one Seattle Mariner baseball game during each home stand. We used to attend many Seahawk football games, but now we like to build a fire at home and watch them on television rather than going out to the game.

One of Chuck's greatest pleasures is woodworking. He has made some wonderful things for the whole family — pine armoires, dressers, bedside tables, shelves, trunks, cribs, cradles, outdoor furniture, TV trays, and so on. He is an excellent craftsman. He named his furniture company "Charlie Crafted," and puts that name on each piece.

Occasionally it's hard to have him out in his workshop. Sometimes I get lonesome just to have him around. This house is so big, we don't often see each other unless we plan to be in the same room. I know that sounds unbelievable, but it's true. When I relax, I like to watch television or read. When Chuck relaxes he likes to DO something. When I watch television I like to watch relationship programs with a good story line. If Chuck watches television he likes *McHale's Navy,* and programs like the old *Sergeant Bilko* series. We taped *War and Remembrance* to be able to watch it together when we had time, and also to fast-forward through the commercials. We enjoyed watching the first episode together, but the second one just had too many relationships in it for Chuck. He wanted more action. So I've been watching the rest of them alone as I knit, while he does something more active.

I know there are many women who would like to have my problem. They want their husbands to get up and do something around the house. So I have to remember this, and I do; but sometimes I wish we enjoyed the same type of entertainment.

Chuck also likes to shop, but we don't like to do the same kind of shopping. When we do go together, we set our watches and shop separately, and meet again at a planned time and place.

I like to swim and lay in the sun. Chuck doesn't like to swim, and seldom even puts on a pair of shorts unless he's playing tennis or pickleball. When we go on trips I never pack his swimming trunks because I know they will not be worn.

Chuck reads a lot. He picks mystery novels, especially science fiction mystery novels. He reads a lot about the New Age Movement, and counseling is one of his favorite topics in the Christian realm. He also likes books on the Civil War, World War II, archaeology, and history.

When I read, I pick relationship novels such as the Zion series by Bodie Thoene. I prefer novels that teach me something. I like biographies and autobiographies of Christian leaders. I like to hear about the personal experiences of others. *Walk Across America* was a favorite. And I'm very interested in anything that helps me learn more about the Bible.

Chuck and I are different. As hard as we try, we seldom like to do the same kind of things. But the Lord said through the apostle Paul that we are to accept one another, just as Christ accepted us. That's the key.

Occasionally our "differentness" gets to both of us. We yearn to have the other one "more like me." When I get tired of it, I remember the Lord's words in Matthew 10:40 — "He who receives you receives Me, and he who receives Me receives Him who sent Me."

I not only need to accept Chuck, but also to *receive* him completely. The Greek here means to receive by deliberate and ready reception of what is offered. In other words, I don't believe I should expect him to change just because I don't like to do all the things he likes to do. The Lord said to love others as He has loved us, which means we are to love others just as they are. I think that we forget to apply that to our marriages as well as to our other relationships. The Lord's instructions on marriage roles are not the only instructions that apply to marriage. Chuck is my brother in Christ as well as my husband, and I am his sister in Christ. All the teachings that tell us how to relate to one another in the church as a whole are to be used in our relationship with each other as well.

Sometimes I REALLY wish he was different, but he feels the same way about me. I know I would not accomplish as much if it were not for Chuck. I know that I need him to push me so I will be all that God wants me to be. To be passive is not always good, just as too much activity is not always good. I know God put us together so we can balance each other. And yet, it's in that balancing that friction and tension come to our relationship.

In the early years we each tried hard to prove we were right. Today it's easier, because we are both willing to give in sooner. We both have the desire to persevere through our trials in a God-honoring way. We've come to the realization that it isn't worth it to lose harmony with each other just to have our own way. We do not agree on many things, and it remains a constant thing that we have to deal with. However, we value our relationship more than we value our own way (most of the time!).

THOUGHTS TO CONSIDER

Do you and your mate like to do the same recreational things, or are you different?

Have you tried to change each other?

Is it all right with you if your interests are different?

Have you tried to enjoy what he enjoys? (It's important to try.)

When you play together, is your attitude good, so he has a good time and doesn't feel he is putting you out?

Have you accepted your mate as God's gift to you to mold you into the image of Jesus Christ?

We are molded in the hard times, not in the good times.

Do you plan to be "playful" and have fun with your husband, knowing he would love to have fun with you?

Does your husband know that you think he is wonderful "just as he is"?

Acceptance allows a person to feel approval, and to respond to you rather than resist you.

SCRIPTURES TO KNOW

ROMANS 14:17-18
For the kingdom of God is not eating and drinking, but righteousness and peace and joy in the Holy Spirit. For he who in this way serves Christ is acceptable to God and approved by men.

JAMES 3:13-18, NIV
Who is wise and understanding among you? Let him show it by his good life, by deeds done in the humility that comes from wisdom. But if you harbor bitter envy and selfish ambition in your hearts, do not boast about it or deny the truth. Such wisdom does not come down from heaven but is earthly, unspiritual, of the devil. For where you have envy and selfish ambition, there you find disorder and every evil practice.

But the wisdom that comes from heaven is first of all pure; then peace-loving, considerate, submissive, full of mercy and good fruit, impartial and sincere. Peacemakers who sow in peace raise a harvest of righteousness.

HIS FUTURE & MINE

And we know with an absolute certainty,
that God causes all things to work together
resulting in good to those who love God,
to those who are called
according to His purpose.
ROMANS 8:28 (*Wuest*)

HOW MANY TIMES have you had this thought: "This marriage is no fun"? Or, "Being a mother is not what I thought it would be"? Or, "I thought this job would be better than it is"? Or, "I'm so tired of doing the same thing over and over again. I don't like my circumstances at all"?

When I was a young wife and mother I heard a pastor on the radio say, "Life is so daily." It's true. Despite what our dreams are and how much we wish our dreams would come true, life IS so daily.

I remember taking a bath one day with bubble bath and the whole works, and especially enjoying the luxurious feeling. After stepping out of the tub I looked back and thought, *You always have to wash the bathtub!*

Life is like that. It's "daily," and you always have to wash the bathtub. That doesn't mean life is drudgery, but it can be if our attitude toward life is not Christlike.

These daily things just ARE. We can fight them, but we can also realize that even though we always have chores like washing bathtubs, we can have a good time doing them too.

Years ago Chuck and I read an article about living for today rather than always living in the future. The writer suggested we tend to think we will be happy "when we get our new house, or "when we have a baby," or "when my mate changes." Some people never seem to enjoy what they are doing NOW. Their real life seems to be somewhere off in the future. And then, if some of their goals come true, it's always another goal that will finally make them happy if they could just attain IT.

We determined, after reading that article, that we would try to live each day in a happy way, without always wishing for more. I know we haven't always been successful, but more times than not we have.

Another belief that helps us live this way is knowing God is in control of every circumstance and happening in our lives. We believe that even what we call "bad times" are ultimately from Him — that He either initiated them or allowed them (Deuteronomy 32:39).

So — if God is in control (and He is), and if He rules over all (and He does), and since we have put our lives into His hands…we know that what is happening in our lives at this moment is from Him.

Psalm 139 states what we believe better than I ever could:

O LORD, you have searched me
    and you know me.

You know when I sit and when I rise;
    you perceive my thoughts from afar.
You discern my going out and my lying down;
    you are familiar with all my ways.
Before a word is on my tongue
    you know it completely, O LORD.

You hem me in — behind and before;
    you have laid your hand upon me.
Such knowledge is too wonderful for me,
    too lofty for me to attain.

Where can I go from your Spirit?
    Where can I flee from your presence?
If I go up to the heavens, you are there;
    if I make my bed in the depths, you are there.
If I rise on the wings of the dawn,
    if I settle on the far side of the sea,
even there your hand will guide me,
    your right hand will hold me fast.

If I say, "Surely the darkness will hide me
    and the light become night around me,"
even the darkness will not be dark to you;
    the night will shine like the day,
    for darkness is as light to you.

For you created my inmost being;
    you knit me together in my mother's womb.
I praise you because I am fearfully and wonderfully made;
    your works are wonderful,
    I know that full well.

My frame was not hidden from you
    when I was made in the secret place.
When I was woven together in the depths of the earth,
    your eyes saw my unformed body.
All the days ordained for me
    were written in your book
    before one of them came to be.

How precious to me are your thoughts, O God!
    How vast is the sum of them!
Were I to count them,
    they would outnumber the grains of sand.
When I awake,
    I am still with you.

If only you would slay the wicked, O God!
    Away from me, you bloodthirsty men!
They speak of you with evil intent;
    your adversaries misuse your name.
Do I not hate those who hate you, O Lord,
    and abhor those who rise up against you?
I have nothing but hatred for them;
    I count them my enemies.

Search me, O God, and know my heart;
    test me and know my anxious thoughts.
See if there is any offensive way in me,
    and lead me in the way everlasting.

This psalm says that God "discerns my going out and my lying down." Another translation puts it, "Thou dost scrutinize my path and my lying down." The Hebrew word translated as "discern" and "scrutinize" means to winnow. When one winnows wheat, the good is separated from the bad. God does the same for us. He takes out of our path everything He does not want to be there, everything He does not want us to go through.

I never would have chosen to go through the hard times Chuck and I have had. And yet, those hard times are the very reason we are able to help others today. If my commitment had been to my happiness at any cost, I probably would not have persevered, and Chuck feels the same. However, our commitment was and is to the Lord first, and then to each other.

When I once told Chuck that I didn't like him very much, but was completely committed to him — that commitment was because I am completely sold out first to Christ.

Chuck and I still have disagreements. We do not always understand each other. But we do our best to serve and accept one another and be all that the Lord wants us to be — for Him, and not for ourselves.

Yes, we fail. But as Chuck has said so often, "Let's just begin again."

Thoughts to Consider

Are you completely committed to Jesus Christ?

Do you want what He wants for your life — no matter what?

Are you willing to persevere through hard times, knowing God has winnowed your path and taken out everything He doesn't want you to go through?

Do you really believe God rules over all?

Will you submit your will to His?

When He heals your hurts, will you help others the way you have been helped?

SCRIPTURES TO KNOW

ROMANS 8:28
And we know that God causes all things to work together for good to those who love God, to those who are called according to His purpose.

JEREMIAH 29:11
"For I know the plans that I have for you," declares the LORD, "plans for welfare and not for calamity, to give you a future and a hope."

ROMANS 8:35-39
Who shall separate us from the love of Christ? Shall tribulation, or distress, or persecution, or famine, or nakedness, or peril, or sword? Just as it is written, "For Thy sake we are being put to death all day long; we were considered as sheep to be slaughtered." But in all these things we overwhelmingly conquer through Him who loved us. For I am convinced that neither death, nor life, nor angels, nor principalities, nor things present, nor things to come, nor powers, nor height, nor depth, nor any other created thing, shall be able to separate us from the love of God, which is in Christ Jesus our Lord.

1 CORINTHIANS 15:58
Therefore, my beloved brethren, be steadfast, immovable, always abounding in the work of the Lord, knowing that your toil is not in vain in the Lord.

MY prayer
is that you will love the Lord
with all your heart, with all your soul,
with all your mind, and with all your strength;

that you will obey His principles out of a heart
overflowing with love and gratitude
for what He has done for you;

and that because of your obedience
you will prove God's will is good,
acceptable, and perfect.

Then I know you will find God's will
to be just what you've always
hoped for.

God bless you as you walk with Him.